GATE

Draws on the pioneering work of Dion Fortune and Christine Hartley to produce an elegant synthesis of potent images, by means of which we can all enter the timeless world of myth.

By the same author
AN INTRODUCTION TO THE MYSTICAL QABALAH

GATE
— OF —
MOON
Mythical and Magical Doorways to the Otherworld

by

ALAN RICHARDSON

THE AQUARIAN PRESS
Wellingborough, Northamptonshire

First published 1984

British Library Cataloguing in Publication Data

Richardson, Alan, 1951-
  Gate of moon.
  1. Witchcraft 2. Magic
  I. Title
  133.4'3 BF1566

ISBN 0-85030-365-6

The Aquarian Press is part of the Thorsons Publishing Group
Printed and bound in Great Britain by
Whitstable Litho Ltd., Whitstable, Kent

Dedication

To Christine Hartley, my friend of ancient days, who inspired this.
To Dolores 'ma littel pet across the waves', who made me get it done.
To A.N. (M & T Ltd) for their constant charm and help.
To Michelle, for 'brightening up my spirites, that were afore full sadde'.

'We must learn to interpret every word, deed and event within our lives as a mysterious dealing between our innermost selves and the very Gods which shadow us.'

Contents

Introduction

Aleister Crowley took his new wife Rose into the King's Chamber of the Great Pyramid. By the light of a single candle placed on the edge of a coffer he began to read an invocation from *The Goetia*. Soon the chamber was 'aglow as if with the brightest tropical moonlight. The pitiful dirty yellow flame of the candle was like a blasphemy...The astral light remained during the whole of the invocation and for some time afterwards...' W.B. Yeats was told by spirits that they had 'come to give him new metaphors for poetry' which resulted in his book *A Vision*. Alfred Watkins, sitting in his car outside the village of Blackwardine had a vision of a Britain that was covered by a web of light – the ley lines which attract so much attention now, 60 years after his pioneering work. Christine Hartley, another student of magic, saw a chalice buried under the hill next to Glastonbury Tor while she was out on the 'inner planes'. Joan Grant, as recorded by her then husband Charles Beatty, while on holiday in Eire, was terrified by a vision of a giant and ancient god wading through a lake. William Gray, while on a dawn pilgrimage to the Rollrights in Oxfordshire, spent an hour or so 'talking' to the stones and exchanging simple yet satisfying information. A woman on an English island drew a sea-king from a deep bay and had her house stinking of seaweed and puddled with brine for days afterward. Men who tried to take aerial photographs of the Gog Magog chalk figures found their camera refused to work at the last moment. Old forestry workers in Cumberland would mutter about 'good' and 'bad' woods in ways that had nothing to do with the quality of timber. While there is a man in Kent, Dusty Miller, who sees the tree-spirits known as dryads and can cajole them into talismans.

There is real magic around. Even though industrialization has ruined the relationships we once had with nature, even though science is taking us into appalling levels of reality and possibility, even though we are nourished by a variety of electronic or narcotic nipples, the magic is still there and the Old Gods are still alive. As long as we remember them they are still alive. And if they want us they will come in and get us whether we wear robes or denim jeans. It makes no difference to them.

So we might state at the outset the attitude of this book: that magic does exist; that people do have remarkable talents in the psychic field which are either trained or hereditary; that an Otherworld exists which can be contacted; and that we can use myth and magic to evolve within. Yet at the same time it cannot be affirmed too strongly that magicians of even the highest order are as prone to the same hurts and disappointments and difficulties as the rest of us. W.B. Yeats spent the best part of a lifetime pursuing Maude Gonne and then her daughter. The occasionally demonic Crowley was incapable of sustaining any kind of relationship. While the essentially benign occultist Dion Fortune, for all her undoubted power, for all her cosmic visions and transcendent experiences, still ended up making a bad marriage with Dr Penry Evans which subsequently ended in divorce. C.R.F. Seymour, a magician who wrote under the initials F.P.D., was a man who inspired enormous devotion, a man of real status in magical terms but who had to reconcile this with marriage to a woman who abhorred anything of the sort. Let us not fool ourselves then, that magicians live on levels of understanding utterly beyond our own ranges. They go through the same things we all go through. Perhaps the only difference is that they recover more quickly.

In reading about the more famous magicians, witches and mystics of this century it is wise to bear in mind the verb coined by Stan Gooch, namely 'to flie'. That is, a lie (or half truth) which has been given wings. Occultists, even the best of them, are guilty of 'flieing' from time to time. Crowley 'flied' higher than just about anyone. Dion Fortune was guilty of this too in parts of her classic *Psychic Self-defence*, although it is said that she was very ill with leukaemia at this time which must excuse a lot. Magicians and their ilk, no matter how much they like to think it, are not scientists. Crowley's piece of doggerel at the front of the *Equinox*: 'We place no reliance on virgin or pigeon/ Our method is Science, our aim is Religion' sums up the common conceit of the

magician. For he is, above all, an artist, and his symbol is the Fool
of the tarot pack who balances on the edge of unknown depths,
traversing the 'debateable lands' between the conscious and
unconscious minds, between this world and the Otherworld, and
stepping from one to the other as the impulse demands. The
really powerful magicians are the grey ones, for the white and
black limit themselves by definition. Prone to the supra-rational
experience magicians can only go so far with their logical
faculties. They make poor philosophers, second-rate academics,
but once they mesh into the Otherworld then they take that
Foolish step off the brink after which they either 'flie' or fly. Or a
bit of both.

This world would be dismal without them.

Crowley was undoubtedly a rogue, a rascal-guru with a severely warped personality and perhaps one tenth of the powers he intimated, if that. Yet there are moments in his life when the newcomer reading his *Confessions* feels himself bristling with excitement. The same holds true of Dion Fortune who wrote:

> I have had my full share of adventures of the Path...seen phenomena such as no seance room has ever known...taken part in psychic feuds...kept the occult vigil when one dare not sleep while the sun is below the horizon; and hung on desperately, matching my staying power against the attack until the moon-tides changed and the force of the onslaught blew itself out.[1]

These people make us feel that they have their hands upon the latch of a gate, a gate between the worlds. They make us feel that if we can only learn to step through this gate we too can stand for a while with stars at elbow and feet, in a place where death has no dominion.

And it is possible.

Magicians, however, tend to make two misassumptions.

The first is that there was once a single and intellectually comprehensible Truth which subsequently became so fragmented as to be almost irretrievable. Almost. Since the printing press and widespread travel has enabled everyone to learn about the diversity of systems, occultists have devoted much time in trying to relate the tarot, to runes, to the I-Ching, to the Hebrew alphabet, to all the Gods and Goddesses. Perhaps there was a Primal Truth, but such efforts in retrieving it are like trying to reconstruct a painting from studying the palette alone; even if we do have to try. It seems that if the Gods have any one law it is that Mystery shall remain. Ena Twigg, the medium, described it as the 'law of frustration' in which, just when all loose ends are being tied up and a definite pattern seen, something comes along which undoes the pattern completely. Occultists are much occupied just now with the researches into the right and left brain theories, as these seem to fit rather well into the various occult anatomies. At the same time research of an equally high level into people who have, technically, no brain at all apparently refutes the whole scheme. There comes a point when it becomes futile to talk in terms of Truth, for something will always come along to deny it in such convincing terms that psychological edifices will crumble. The writer A.J. Stewart, for example, claims to be the reincarnation of James IV, King of Scots, and presents her case in two superb books *Falcon* and *Died 1513, Born 1929* (an appalling title but one chosen by her publishers against her wishes). Personally, I have no doubt whatsoever that she was who she claims. And yet I cannot begin to answer Ian Wilson's criticism of her in his study *Reincarnation*, in which he shows that modern X-ray techniques have refuted a statement Ms Stewart made concerning a Holbein painting.[2] In the same way I have no doubt that Dr Arthur Guirdham once had a past life in the Languedoc in the thirteenth century, although I cannot accept his 'far memories' of a much earlier life in the Mediterranean during the latter days of the Eleusinian Mysteries.[3] Likewise, Joan Grant's *Winged Pharoah* convinces me that she has been an illuminated Egyptian princess, though her *Return to Elysium* leaves me cold. I myself believe that I had a life in the English Middle March of the Borders during the Middle Ages, but confess to nothing remotely resembling proof of this. Nor am I particularly concerned with looking for it. Like Guirdham's Cathars, if the past wants to come looking for someone then it will, without much consideration for their thoughts in the matter. These personal visions are part of each soul's 'myth' without which our lives remain ordinary, even a little desperate. The late W.E. Butler who wrote one excellent book on magic and several indifferent ones noted that we must hold lightly on to things and jettison them without a qualm, if necessary. So I choose to believe in reincarnation because I choose to believe in reincarnation, and not because of any philosophical reasoning or startling far memories. As one of the Greek philosophers said, life without Mystery would become meaningless.

So the other misassumption is that we must try to analyse magic in scientific terms, to try and make it respectable. Perhaps it would be better if the magician simply got on with his rituals and let the scientists come toward him. Which they will.

The scientist tries to examine the real nature of the photograph; he tries to get away from the psychological configuration, the meaning of the image, to move down to some other more basic level of patterns of alternating dots of light and dark, a world of elementary

particles. And yet what does he find there but another mental
configuration, another arrangement of psychological meaning? If he
persists in this direction long enough, the mythological dimensions
of science will become apparant in his work, as they would have if he
had asked himself questions about the meaning of sunlight rather
than questions about the behaviour of photons.

Science wrought to its uttermost becomes myth. History wrought
to its uttermost becomes myth. [1]

Magic is the antidote to the stultifying aspects of science in many
cases. It is poetry and dream. It may well be a placebo but the fact
is that it works. As long as writers such as Colin Wilson and Stan
Gooch continue to point out to occultists generally when they
might be 'flieing', there is no need to seek respectability in
scientific circles. Dom Robert Petitpierre OSB, exorcized his
demons through an absolute faith in his Lord and the rites of the
Church. There was no question in his mind but that he would
triumph for he was acting in the name of the All-powerful. Had
he ever stopped to subject his rites and prayers to scientific
scrutiny then those demons — whatever they were — would have
shredded his soul. How could any entity resist such power?

The fact is that *anything* can be made to work. Krishnamurti,
when asked about the mantras doled out by the teachers of 'TM',
said rather acidly that one can achieve just as exalted levels of
consciousness by intoning 'coca-cola' with intensity. Those occult
groups which hint at Great Secrets based upon a lost science
should not fool anyone, for there is no One Truth in magic, no
supreme system. It is not even necessary in fact to make robes,
wands, or create a temple in the spare room in which to invoke
angels. No robed magician in his circle ever invoked the 'solar-
phallic' current as powerfully as D.H. Lawrence, whose writings
had a definite and profound effect upon our century. While no
naked practitioner of the Craft ever called upon the Earth Mother
as potently as John Cowper Powys whose work was done in
trains, boats and in his sitting-room.

The aim of this book then, is to build a gate of Moon, just as
some gates are made of wood or iron. Those occultists with an eye
for poetic truth choose to regard the Moon as a hole in the sky
through which light from the Otherworld pours. Nice, that. The
Moon is a symbol of the unconscious, of the astral light, of

dreams, of instinctual drives. By using myths which draw upon these qualities we can thus fashion a Gate of Moon whose latch is operable by ourselves alone. The ones that will specifically concern us are those fundamental to the Western psyche, and little attempt will be made to sift down through the layers to discern some kind of original. Levi-Strauss wrote:

> This has been one of the main obstacles to the progress of mythological studies, namely, the quest for the true version, or the earlier one. On the contrary, we define myth as consisting of all its versions; to put it otherwise: a myth remains the same as long as it is felt as such.[5]

It makes no difference whether Malory or Nennius or Chretien de Troyes expressed the 'purest' version, as it is all valid material for our gate. Though what we do when the gate is built — whether we simply knock politely or leap boldly through — is another matter.

THE MOON.

1.

Old Gods and Other Contacts

The best thing about myth is that there is so much of it. It renews itself hourly. It is ever-becoming and self-perpetuating, a source of boundless energy if it can be tapped. We dream it, we live it. We have only to align ourselves with any poignant myth and the eyes of our psyches expand a little, we take in more light and see better in the dark. We no longer bump into things with quite as much frequency or force because we can often anticipate them surging out of the gloom as we fumble along.

It is only a matter of finding the right myth. Carl Jung knew a Pueblo Indian chief named Ochwiay Biano who was responsible for the sun rising each morning. The chief knew the world would collapse if he did not perform the necessary rites. He did them not only for himself but for all men. He was a very wise man. There was a footballer in Manchester who was, briefly, an Orpheus incarnate who could make people sing in their hearts; naturally he got lost in the underworld and never quite emerged. While once I had an *hierosgamos* thrust upon me in a small room in Kentucky between a hamburger joint and a pancake house, and I became Osiris and she became Isis while the gods looked down and the lightning flashed outside and rain came in under the door.

For the masses the Christian myth was given as a pattern. We all have moments of betrayal, we have little crucifixions, sometimes daily; we have all been Judas to someone and Doubting Thomases to someone else. The Christian epic is there for us to focus upon ourselves if we so wish, and it tells us that there are times when we must have the courage to draw circles in the dust and stand in them, protecting whatever whorish belief we hold, against the stones of an angry mob.

Magicians are connoisseurs of myths. They not only collect them but use them. Yeats, who was an adept within the now-

legendary Order of the Golden Dawn, went around Ireland with
Lady Gregory and others collecting the peasants' tales of the Old
Gods. But while most, like the young American student Evans-
Wentz, were content to amass these for publication and thus
preservation, Yeats was back home in his tower, Thoor Ballylee,
working on the creation of a Castle of Heroes, a ritual centre
where the Celtic gods could be invoked once more.

Magicians have their Qabalah to help them of course, and the
Tree of Life glyph with its ten categories capable of infinite
interpretation, but yet fixed in a definite pattern around a specific
centre. The images thus relate in a definite manner without, in a
sense, flying off into space like fragments of shrapnel never to be
reassembled. The centre of this glyph is the sphere Tiphereth,
which means Beauty and Harmony, and equates with the sun. So
the magicians have, at the very heart of their mythological and
magical systems, a brilliant central light from which all things
radiate. More of the Qabalah later.

We must take the sun as a beginning, therefore, D.H.
Lawrence, who was surely a priest of Mithras in a previous life,
virtually concluded his writing career with the words: 'Start with
the sun, and the rest will slowly, slowly happen.' The planets
were formed from the molten gases flung from that orb. Someday
they will fall back into it. It is obviously a heavenly body of
paramount importance to us. What we must do is 'set our controls
for the heart of the sun' as the song has it, find our centres and
then begin to radiate outward. Although it is not so much that we
can find these centres through any conscious techniques of self-
knowledge but that life itself will hammer us into shape around
our radiant cores.

In the system of correspondences used by magicians the sun
relates to figures such as Jesus, Horus, Baldur, and to all those
gods who died and rose again for our illumination. These are
what James Frazer called the 'Sacrificed Gods'. As we have noted
there is a Sacrificed God at the very centre of Western
consciousness who has given energy to our whole civilization for
two thousand years. Magicians for the most part have used this
Judaeo-Christian tradition as the basis for their magical imagery
for some time now, but the world is changing in such a way that
something else is needed.

What is proposed here is the creation of a magical system based around a different solar figure. Ideally this figure should be one in the tradition of Sacrificed Gods, a strong central character, wise, wondrous, brilliant, strong, priestly, and capable of inspiring beauty and love in a way that will captivate the Western psyche.

It is Arthur of course. *Rex Quondam Rex Futurus*. The Once and Future King. He had a miraculous conception and mysterious upbringing. He gathered around him a circle of men who imposed a new and exalted ethic upon a nation. The spiritual impulse behind his Court, the quest for the Holy Grail, still obsesses us. He sacrificed himself for his country but did not quite die, being carried off to Avalon until such a time as he would be needed again. He was a wonder-child, priest-king and Sacrificed God. He will come again. He has never been away.

The other figures within the cycle are just as important. Merlin, Nimue, Lancelot, Mordred, and Guinevere represent nodes of collective consciousness which we can tap and which we express unwittingly at every moment. When a boy first falls in love then it is Nimue he sees, smiling up at him from the depths of a pool. Whenever we use our intelligence to resolve some problem then it is Merlin's robe we don. Anyone who has ever

THE HANGED MAN.

been cuckolded becomes Arthur. Presently we will study each image in detail and see how they affect us on every level from the physical through the magical to the spiritual.

In terms of the magical, spasmodic efforts have been to work an 'Arthurian' system by many individuals and groups. The Fraternity of the Inner Light, formed by Dion Fortune, once had a section of its headquarters set aside specifically for these aspects of the British Mysteries, although only fragments of these come through in her published writings. She herself lived at the foot of Glastonbury Tor next to Chalice Well associated with human sacrifice and the shade of Morgan le Fay. She was obviously miffed by the novelist John Cowper Powys' approach to the Arthurian Mystery yet, on a different plane, his *A Glastonbury Romance* calls up the spirit of the place as well as her rituals ever did. Occult knowledge and techniques are not obligatory for insight, and in differing ways we can all become Merlin while at the same time learning to see him appear in others.

Although Fortune's group has apparently, since her death in 1946, moved away from such matters toward the teachings of Alice Bailey and her 'Tibetan', there is a descendant organization known as the 'Servants of the Light', founded by the late W.E. Butler. The entire impulse of this group is Arthurian, involving a programme of self-initiation by systematically creating a Grail Castle within the imagination. A Gate of Moon, in fact, through which one can come and go.

To forestall any conclusions, I do not, never have, and never will belong to any occult organization. My own connection with these images in occult fields is through Morgan le Fay herself. I met her for the first time in 1978 on a bright but cold day in November. My first wife and I pulled into the gravel drive outside her lovely house in Hampshire and she came out to greet us. She was exactly as I had imagined her, although not so tall. She was in her eighties, looked to be in her sixties, and her mind had a sharpness which could lacerate mine. Silver hair and blue eyes, she had the knowing face and prescience of a sybil, a priestess secure within her Mystery. I have rarely felt so much at ease with another person.

This was Christine Hartley of course, who trained under Dion Fortune before going on to work at the highest levels with Colonel Seymour, or 'Kim' as he was known to his intimates. To

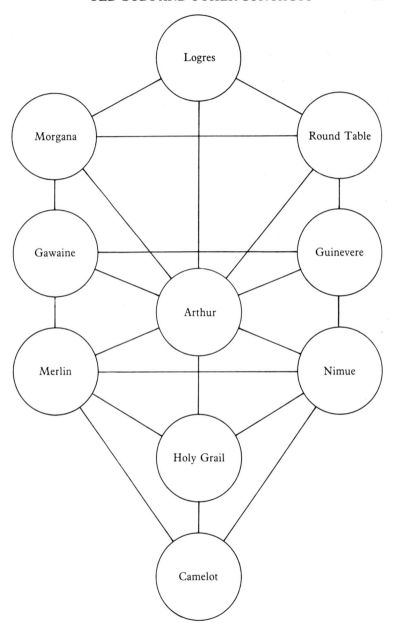

use an Eastern term, she was his *shakti*. It was through her books, *A Case for Reincarnation*, and the *Western Mystery Tradition*, that I came to write to her. She had mentioned in the latter that Northumberland, my native county, had been a druidic stronghold. Naturally I wanted to know more, and was pleased to learn that her late husband had also shared my passion for this area. While in *A Case for Reincarnation* she gave fascinating details of her work with Dion Fortune, especially of the magical seership she practised under the Colonel, or F.P.D. as he is referred to throughout. To her, Arthur, Merlin and Morgan were titles handed down through the generations. So there have been countless Arthurs and innumerable Merlins, as we shall discuss later. As she saw it Morgan was one of the 'sea-borne' priestesses who came to Britain when Atlantis was destroyed.

> Because I was one of the young priestesses and had work to do in another place, when the destruction of Atlantis was known to be approaching I was put into a small boat with F.P.D. and a few other people... and we were eventually washed up on the coast of Lyonesse after being tossed about on a raging sea.[1]

She was not the only one however, for she insists that Morgan was a generic name and that there were cycles of Morgans and cycles of Merlins. Interestingly, although she would make no comment on this when I taxed her, there is a strong parallel between this and Dion Fortune's novel *The Sea Priestess*. In point of fact Christine acted as an editor for many of Fortune's manuscripts, and if *The Sea Priestess* and *Moon Magic* are at all readable today then it is due in no small part to her efforts.

I have seen Morgan-as-Christine many times since. I have seen her in other women too. But I saw her once in an entirely different guise. We used to live in a small basement flat overlooking a deep and narrow valley in Somerset. One evening I stood upon the veranda watching the valley fill with shadows like a lake as the sun fell, a thin silver moon arose, and the stars came out in a violet sky. It was one of those dusks in late summer when the air seems to throb like a slow drum and suddenly there doesn't seem to be much difference between the worlds at all. Gradually I began to feel certain that Morgan was in the valley looking up at me – that Morgan *was* the valley. I felt a call in my head like the sea sucking back through rounded stones...

This is Morgan too. I have been down into that valley a thousand times and seen nothing more wondrous than a few cows, a few houses, the usual picnic rubbish... but I know that she is there, all around. If I had answered her call that night I would in some sense have met her. But I didn't, my wife called me back in for supper and I went. Sometimes that sort of thing is even more important than answering goddesses. Morgan understands, in that hard way of hers.

If this is an idiosyncratic way of studying the ancient gods then let it be so. It cannot be said too often that magic is not the province of an elite blessed with supreme insight and astounding psychism. As Crowley said 'Magick is for All', though he went the wrong way about showing this.

2.

Witch Queens and Cauldrons

In the beginning was the Mother, and the Mother was a goddess, and the Mother was *the* goddess. No-one knows her name, and so we can call her what we will. James Vogh calls her Arachne, the spider-goddess, the lost and thirteenth sign of the zodiac. We may as well call her Isis, Binah or Morgan, for they are all one. At one time the Mother was supreme. As Aldous Huxley said somewhere: 'To palaeolithic man every day was Mother's day.' In a sense Western civilization is a history of the struggle between matriarchal and patriarchal systems. With the Mother being dethroned. It has left the magicians and mystics yearning for the ancient times with the same wistfulness that old men show for the good old days. And yet in an odd way, by being dethroned, she has actually gained in power in other areas.

As to how this displacement of the feminine occurred we can only make conjectures. Which is invariably far more accurate and valid than consulting the so-called 'akashic records' beloved of the Theosophists especially. Merlin Stone, commenting on the Middle East at a time when the worship of Inanna, Ishtar and Astarte was supreme, wrote:

> From the point of view of those who followed the religion of the Goddess, they were simply carrying out the ancient ways. From the point of view of the invading Hebrew tribes, the older religion was now to be perceived as an orgiastic, evil, lustful, shameful, disgraceful, sinful, base fertility-cult. But may we suspect that underlying this *moral* stance was the political manoeuvering for power over land and property accessible to them only upon institution of a patrilineal system? [1]

After all, in any society where an orgiastic fertility-cult is of central importance, the *paternity* of children could never be proven. And so attempts to impose a patrilineal system must necessarily begin with the subjection of the feminine, and strict rules imposed on marriage and procreation. In time goddesses such as Astarte became proscribed as demonic, while Yahweh, once a very small and local god indeed, assumed the proportions of the One and Only God. Though as we said this has not diminished the effectiveness of the Mother image for us today. As Jung wrote in his *Mysterium Coniunctionis:*

> The disappearance of the feminine element, namely the cult of the Mother...was all that was needed for the spirituality of the... image to detach itself from earthly man and gradually sink into the unconscious. When such great and significant images fall into oblivion they do not disappear from the human sphere, nor do they lose their psychic power.[2]

Indeed not. As William Irwin Thompson shows in his beautiful book, *The Time Falling Bodies Take to Light*, the feminine compensation for this shift in the natural balance of things is to alter the sexual emphasis from fertility, or reproductive power, to erotic power. Or power over the lover rather than the child.

> Gone is the obese Great Goddess; come is the sleek young maid, the Queen of Heaven. What we now encounter in the male order of civilisation is 'sexiness', the erotic power of the beautiful woman to lure the powerful man to his own destruction. Inanna becomes the archetype for all the Cleopatras to come; she is the 'bitch goddess' who from her first appearance in Sumerian civilisation will live on in all other civilisations – in myth and legend, novel and poem...[3]

She lives on through Morgan, too, the Witch-queen and sister/seducer of the King. Though she is not a Great Mother in the creatress sense, she is certainly the mother of the British Mysteries with a pedigree which can be identified and confirmed by the standards of the Qabalah. In general terms Christine Hartley waxes quite lyrical about her:

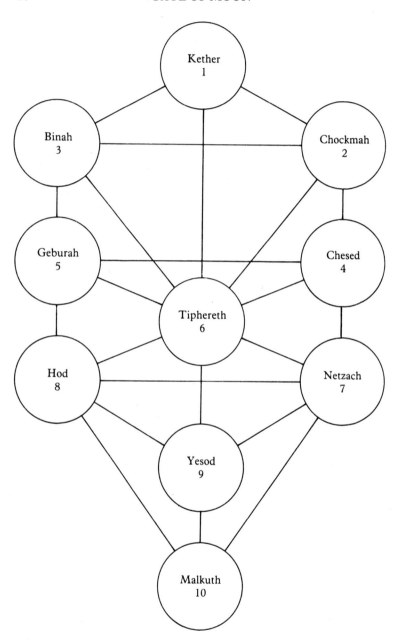

She is the ever-hidden one, the shadowy woman who stands behind giving of her power from the inner planes. She is the feminine principle of the great Triangle of King, Priest and Priestess... she teaches men to work with power; she is Binah on the Tree of Life, the great Mother of form through whom is the manifestation of force.[4]

Now before we go on to look more closely at this dark lady let us describe a little about Binah.

Binah is the third sphere on the Tree of Life. It means Understanding. Associated with this sphere too is the planet Saturn, and the spiritual experience known as the Vision of Sorrow is attributed. Traditional titles given to Binah include: Ama, the dark sterile Mother; Aima, the bright fertile Mother; and Marah, the Great Sea. As we shall see, Morgan fits all of these rather well.

At first it seems that there is a great and irreconcilable contradiction here implied in the titles of bright fertile Mother and dark sterile Mother. Yet all of the primordial figures of the feminine contain these opposites.

As the distance between the conscious and unconscious increases...it frequently happens that the opposites contained in the Great Mother image split apart. We then get a good fairy and a wicked fairy, or a benevolent goddess and one who is malevolent and dangerous. In Western antiquity...the opposites often remain united in the same figure, though this paradox does not disturb the primitive mind in the least.[5]

So it is at this level that we encounter the concept of the Eternal Virgin and Cosmic Whore embodied within the same person. The Great Mother is always regarded as virgin despite the fact that she has many lovers and is the mother of many children. In the Christian Bible the Greek word *parthenos*, which was commonly translated as Virgin, means no more than an unmarried woman. Not necessarily the same thing at all. It seems that in the ancient sense the word virgin simply connoted an unwed person. As regards the Virgin Mary, the magician William Gray gives some very recondite lore in connection with the Immaculate Conception, hinting that this was achieved by means of a primitive form of artificial insemination applied to the

specially chosen candidate. Whatever the source of Gray's idea it
oddly anticipates a similar finding by John M. Allegro in one of
his many tilts at orthodox Christianity.

Now regardless of whether the hymen was broken by natural or
artificial means we must clearly see the condition of virginity as
psychological rather than physical. Both Esther Harding and Jean
Markale analyse this question of virginity in detail, in their books
Women's Mysteries and *Women of the Celts* respectively. To them
the concept means being 'one-in-herself', or 'enclosed upon
herself'. That is, the woman or goddess is not a mere pendant to a
man but is a unique and separate entity in her own right, as
Morgan le Fay could never be regarded as dependant upon
anyone but herself.

> She is the goddess of sexual love but not of marriage. There is no
> male god who as a husband rules her conduct or determines her
> qualities... She is not related to any god as wife or 'counterpart'. She
> is her own mistress, virgin, one-in-herself. The characteristics of
> these great and powerful goddesses do not mirror those of any of the
> male gods, nor do they represent the feminine counterpart of
> characteristics originally male... for they represent the essence of the
> feminine in sharpest contrast to the essence of masculinity.[6]

Though it may be Morgan or one of her ilk who first stimulates
the primordial forces within a person, we can never entrap that
goddess, for she would destroy us.

This is where we come to the black side, the Dark Sterile
Mother aspect of Morgan, though these are not qualities so
remote that we rarely, if ever, see them. Edging off the bright face
we present to the world and ourselves there is a fluctuating grey
border, a debateable land which acts as a buffer zone against the
darkness. It comes through to us sometimes. Usually it leaks
across in small amounts and then we feel a sense of foreboding, or
doom. At a more intense level it becomes what Dylan Thomas
called his 'black dog', a bristling, howling wild beast which is
destructive of friendships and indeed anything which enters its
territory. When this mood comes through in force it is curiously
intense and almost erotically savage. There is a complete
indifference to the law, society and death, the sort of fury which
overtook the Viking baresarkers. War, of course, brings it through

more surely than any other stimulus. Michael Herr in his superb book *Despatches* captures the essence of the unspeakable impulses which cause men to go back into battle again and again even when they are no longer compelled to do so. Phillip Caputo in his *Rumor of War* said that he was never more intensely alive than in combat. Perhaps because he was using the whole of himself during those times instead of forever keeping a lid upon the welling darkness. When we try to deny this side – the 'shadow' as Jung called it – then we emasculate ourselves. Morgan is a death-goddess. Her symbol is a raven, that bird which kills sheep by biting out the tongue, pecking out the eyes, and then ripping open the stomach. We are all sheep.

An acceptance of death, however, gives us freedom. An understanding of Morgan gives us a comparable shift of viewpoint. Kahlil Gibran wrote in *The Prophet*:

> When you are joyous, look deep into your heart and you shall find it is only that which has given you sorrow which is giving you joy.
> When you are sorrowful look again into your heart, and you shall see that in truth you are weeping for that which has been your delight.[7]

Gibran understood that sorrow and darkness are necessary, and that we can learn from them. We must sing to Morgan as don Juan Matus and don Genaro danced in praise of their Death, in Castaneda's interesting novels.

My own death-omen is a raven. The dilemma was having either an Old Woman in Black appear, or a raven, and I chose the latter. More room for it to come tapping on my windowsill. When my times comes three ravens will appear. We can choose what death-omen we want, if any, and work at it. The raven of Saturn and Morgan is mine.

However we must not dwell too obsessively upon this dark side of Morgan. As an expression of All-Woman she must necessarily contain the dark and bright sides, or *Ama* and *Aima* as the Qabalists would describe it. Perhaps the fullest description of her appearance of character is contained in the *Estoire de Merlin*:

> She was the sister of King Arthur, very gay and playful; she sang most agreeably; though dark in the face, very well made, neither too fat nor too thin, with beautiful hands, perfect shoulders, skin softer than silk, engaging of manner, long and straight in the body: altogether wonderfully seductive and, besides all that, the warmest and most sensual woman in all Great Britain. Merlin had taught her astronomy and many other things, and she studied them so well that she became an excellent scholar and was later called Morgan La Fee because of the marvels she wrought. She expressed herself with delightful sweetness, and was more good-natured and attractive than anyone else in the world, when she was calm. But when her anger was aroused... she was very difficult to appease...[8]

This can provide what magicians would call a magical image. We can use this. Visualize one of the massive trilithons of Stonehenge – a very saturnine place. Place yourself before it so that the stones loom above you, awesome. Beyond this gate is Morgan, beckoning from her twilight world. There are willow trees behind her. In her left hand she holds the miraculous scabbard she once stole from Arthur. In the sky, just above the rocky, bleak horizon is the ringed planet itself. See yourself step through and reach toward Morgan's outstretched hand...

This exercise should not be done lightly, no matter how seductive Morgan's image. The Morganic contact can take many forms and is not necessarily immediately benign. Life might suddenly become difficult; odd things might rise to the surface, frightening things. We might come to see her as a purely evil creature. Yet as Heinrich Zimmer points out: '...the experience of evil, and to some extent this experience alone, produces maturity, real life, real command of the powers and tasks of life.' The Morganic contact is not for the naïve and innocent. The more experience one has of the shadow-side of the psyche before approaching her, the safer it is to do so and the more beautiful she appears. To state it esoterically, if one can learn to love the Black Isis first, then she will change into the White Isis of far greater beauty than can be experienced by a shallow adoration of the White Isis alone. Dion Fortune expresses this point in her novel *Moon Magic*:

> Great Isis built up, the terrible Black Isis, the source of all power, who seldom comes, and only at great moments. I am used to Her power and received it fearlessly, knowing that in a few seconds She would change into Her beautiful aspect, which is so much more beautiful than anything that can be built under the symbolism of the White Isis, who is always liable to change over into the Black Isis if much power is brought through Her. Therefore we who have knowledge work with the Black Isis and transmute Her.[9]

We can thus equate Morgan with Isis, and also with Kali, the terrible death-goddess with the necklace of skulls, as Fortune goes on to say:

> Some equate the Black Isis with Kali, and say that She is evil; but I do not think she is, unless one counts elemental force as evil, which I do not. She is indeed the Breaker in Pieces, but then She sets free. She is also most ancient Life, and people fear the primordial as they fear nothing else. She is a resevoir of tremendous and dynamic force, and when dynamic force comes welling up, that is She.[10]

Which brings us back to the idea of Morgan/Isis/Kali being the initiating and transforming woman, or force. We have all invoked 'Morgan the Red' as she is sometimes called, when we have touched upon the deeper sexual elements of our natures, or else had our consciousness pressed into a tight foetal ball by some tragedy. We cannot avoid these things. They are the *true* initiations over and above the ritual dramas. We have spouses or partners, we have children or careers, joys and burdens. What can any robed Magus give that is more valid than the self-learnt maturity to deal with these? Make your way toward Morgan first, and worry about occult initiations later. But be aware that this goddess is like the Ruby Tuesday of Jagger's song in that 'she comes and then she goes', and no-one can really predict her return, or even be sure where she came from in the first place. D.H. Lawrence expresses something of this in his short story *The Man Who Died*, which tells of a brief relationship with a priestess of Isis and a Jesus who did *not* die upon the cross, a theme which echoes some underground lore to be discussed in later chapters.

It was this hierosgamos, or magical mating, which parallels that which occurred between Arthur and Morgan, and it is interesting to note that this union between brother and sister is virtually universal in its usage. Thus the mating between Morgan and Arthur is but a restatement in British terms of the union between Pharoah and his sister. In larger terms Isis was sister and wife to Osiris; Hera sister and wife to Zeus; Conchobar mated with his sister Dechtire, while Gwyddyon and his sister Arianrod produced the child Lleu Llaw Gyffes.

The significance of the offspring in these cases is something that will be discussed later.

Some sources give Morgause as the one who mated with Arthur and begat Mordred, but we can regard her as another aspect of Triple Goddess symbolism, and thus a more benign aspect of Morgan herself. The latter was one of three sisters, the other two being Morgause and Elaine. There are other parallels within Western mythology relevant to our studies here, as Graves describes in his *White Goddess*:

> The Copts even ventured to combine 'the Three Maries' who were spectators of the Crucifixion into a single character, with Mary Cleopas as a type of 'Blodeuwedd', the Virgin of 'Arianrhod', and Mary Magdalen as the third person of this ancient trinity, who appears in Celtic legend as Morgan le Faye...Morgan in Irish legend is 'the Morrigan', meaning 'Great Queen', a Death-goddess who assumed the form of a raven; and 'le Faye' means 'the Fate'. According to Cormac's *Glossary* the Morrigan was invoked in battle by an imitation on war-horns of a raven's croaking. She was by no means the gentle character familiar to readers of the *Morte D'Arthur* but like the 'black screaming hag Cerridwen' [11]

So we can extend it more: Morgan is the Morrigan is the Magdalen is Keridwen is Isis is Kali. Now let us look at the Welsh aspect for a while.

Keridwen

The earlier name of this goddess was Creiddylad which means 'Daughter of the Sea', as Morgan means 'born of the sea'. She is most commonly associated with her famous cauldron which seems to have been one of the major prototypes of the Grail. Basically the main story in connection with Keridwen is as follows...

Keridwen had three children, one of them, by the name Avaggdu, was a particularly ugly creature whom she intended to cure of this affliction. The means of doing this was by concocting a mixture in her cauldron, which was warmed by the breath of nine maidens. After boiling up the mixture, aimed at inspiration and knowledge, for one whole year she asked Gwyon Bach to watch over it. However three drops of the magic brew fell out of the cauldron onto Gwyon's finger who involuntarily licked this scalded digit and thus attained the perfect knowledge intended for Avaggdu. Needless to say that after such effort Keridwen was furious when she found out the mistake, and the virago appeared within her as she set chase to Gwyon. This chase took on a peculiarly magical nature: Gwyon, to avoid her, changed into a hare, whereupon she became a greyhound; he became a fish, she became an otter; he became a bird and she a hawk; finally he became a grain of corn and she ate him. However this was not the end of the tale for she became pregnant and later gave birth to the beautiful child whom she named Taliesin. So beautiful was this child that she did not have the heart to kill him but instead set him adrift in a small coracle upon the ocean.

It is possible that this tale is descriptive of one of the druidic rituals. Taliesin himself describes how he has been 'thrice-born': of his natural mother, of Keridwen, and of the coracle. Being born of Keridwen brings us back to the idea of the Mother-goddess being an initiating and transforming woman, the latter being exemplified by the constant shape-shifting during the chase of Gwyon. Lewis Spence in his *Mysteries of Britain* goes on to quote Taliesin is saying: 'I was modelled into the form of a pure man in the hall of Keridwen...' Now in the Qabalah the sphere of Binah, or Saturn, is known as the Sphere of Form: 'She is the archetypal womb through which life comes into manifestation. Whatsoever provides a form to serve life as a vehicle is of Her.' So with Keridwen like Morgan, as a Binah figure too, it is apt that Taliesin should state that the form of a 'pure man' – not yet corrupted on the lower planes – should be modelled in the hall of Keridwen. Further, the bard in question ends that statement with '... Keridwen, who subjected me to penance.' To our perceptions the binding and limiting of Keridwen's actions must seem like pure penance, even though it is this which enables us to evolve, as has already been noted. This 'hall' of course, is the womb from which Taliesin was born, or rather re-born.

The cauldron, to study the images further, is an appropriate symbol for both the womb and the vagina. It receives, it holds, and life comes out of it. One can understand the importance of large, communal cauldrons within primitive tribes: the control of fire, the development of agriculture, both altered the old hunting/gathering patterns of early man and eventually, in most societies, the women were left to tend the fire, raise the babies and prepare the food. Perhaps a feminist would interpret this differently. At any rate from the cauldrons which were later built came food prepared by those women not advanced in pregnancy, not tied down with children, and generally free to assume the role within the group of 'cauldron maiden'. To an extent the cauldron symbolizes stability and ease. With a container for water of this size there was no need for such frequent journeys down to the river. In the Iron Age it became either a symbol of the tribe's skill, or its wealth. It is hardly surprising that in the innumerable cauldron myths they are almost always connected with the idea of plenty, of universal nourishment. At times food aplenty seemed to come out of the tribal cauldron, and in the dregs of water left there was always the hope that there might yet be more nourishment hidden in the depths. Just as life came from the cauldron so it came from the womb. All of this is depicted in the goddess Keridwen, who also has the aspect of Earth-mother, to be appeased for the sake of good crops.

An interesting point is that in many accounts the brew contained in her Cauldron of Inspiration is completely poisonous, save for the three drops imbibed by Gwyon; while she is, moreover, regarded as goddess of the Underworld. One analysis of this is that while her outer appearance suggests she may fulfill our lives, she is poison and death to us all. Which of course brings us back to the image of the ever-desirable but ever deadly Morgan the Red.

This sphere with which we are concerned equates with Saturn which equates with Time. Both Morgan and Keridwen have shape-shifting qualities. We ourselves must learn to shape-shift as we get through the days, altering our modes of action and reaction into whatever styles will enable us to survive. It is significant that Gwyon finally changed into a grain of corn, something static and immobile but with immense potential. What is being said here is that our fate will swallow us eventually; we must accept these fate-goddesses and be willing to undergo the symbolic death, the entry into the dark of Keridwen's womb. Yet once we have retreated back to the innermost seed of our innermost nature, then we will have the chance to grow into what we were meant to be in the first place, just as Gwyon became a seed and grew into the marvellous Taliesin. Saturn will drive us into the hell of Keridwen's Underworld, it will also give us the strength to find our way back to the light of our true form. Keridwen, as much as Morgan, is peculiarly appropriate to this Saturn-Binah linkage: for one thing the god Saturn is known for having swallowed his children just as Keridwen swallowed Gwyon; for another, the constant shape-shifting in her chase indicates the ever-ceaseless change inherent in the flow of cyclical Time. Morgan too is an important Time-figure in that she gave birth to Mordred who brought all Britain crashing down, thus ending an era and bringing tragedy to the fore.

So, in brief, Keridwen and Morgan both express the nature of Saturn in that they are Death-goddesses, Time-goddesses, and generally offer us either destruction, or the chance of renewal in better form.

At these levels of divinity however we are yet concerned only with the *idea* of form, rather than form itself; it is the *idea* of womanhood rather than womanhood itself. Morgan is archetypal or prototypal in that the invisible chemical structure finds its way down to more concrete levels where it manifests as a crystal of particular shape and form. Thus when we touch upon the ancient aspects of our inner nature we touch upon Morgan: but even so it is only the hem of her dress that we touch. In practical terms we approach her in roundabout ways, via other gates: we see her beckoning through the gate of instinct and the moon-forces; and through the gate of passion ruled by Nimue. Keridwen too can be seen through the same openings, and also through the earth-gate in her aspect of the British Ceres. So Morgan le Fay, the Great Witch and Great Bitch is found reflected in the realms of Venus, the Moon, and the Earth, and it is through the passionate sex and sensation of the body that we will eventually be propelled into the mysteries of the Great Goddesses.

3.

Heroes, Circles and Standing Stones

Light travels from the sun at measurable but unimaginable speed. It curves. And could we follow this curve we might imagine it as circling back to the same point.

A circle might be described as being composed of an infinite number of infinitely small straight lines fixed about a single point.

Lines of light, Circles of light. A circle of Light. Which gives us the glyph of the Round Table, that body of men wedded to an ideal.

If the last chapter dealt with cauldrons and feminity, with darkness and the womb, this chapter is to do with wands and spears and masculinity, with radiance and the phallus, with standing stones, serpents, and spines.

Teilhard de Chardin, approaching the topic from a different direction and without using mythological imagery to tie his ideas down, summed up the over-all concept:

> The earth is covering itself not merely with millions of thinking units, but with a single continuum of thought, and finally forming a functionally single Unit of Thought of planetary dimensions. The plurality of individual thoughts combine...in a single act of unanimous Thought...In the dimensions of Thought, like the dimension of Time and Space, can the Universe reach consummation in anything but the measureless? [1]

This was the unity of thought achieved on a microcosmic scale when the Round Table was functioning at its best. This was – is – the zodiac. It was Merlin, the British Thoth, who helped find the knights for the places around the Table, and when this was complete, barring the Seige Perilous, we have de Chardin's 'unity of thought', the model of all groups of like-minded individuals whether these groups are occult, sporting, or social.

The Table is an image of Collective Wisdom, with the entire range of experience as expressed by the zodiac revolving around a central point. Perhaps it is from this that we can derive the rod and straight line symbolism that we will deal with shortly: the rod is the axle upon which the Great Wheel turns. It is motionless yet source of all motion, containing the essence of the universe within its core. When the magician stands at the centre of his circle he is concerned with more than the few feet from the middle to the edge: in his exalted belief he is at the centre of the very cosmos, the stars whirl around him. This was the the position Arthur found himself in, as the pole star around which the others revolved.

In the field of the Qabalah we are concerned with the sphere of Chockmah, the primary Male figure. The traditional 'magical image' is that of a bearded male: 'the father who has proved his manhood, not the untried virgin.' Which echoes one of the stipulations for admisssion to the Round Table in that the knight concerned had to have proved himself in some way, on some adventure or Quest. A knight by very definition is in any case a man who has proved himself in the preparatory trials and training, by nature a fighting man, skilled in arms, skilled at riding, able to handle power wisely. Which is more than can be said for most magicians, although to be fair they don't wear as much armour.

The noble ideal of the Round Table is found again and again throughout history. More recently we have seen it expressed in the League of Nations and the United Nations – laudable but doomed impulses. Similarly in the occult groups which are endemic to our societies. Such structures rarely last long – rarely through more than two new leaders and changes of style — after which they seem to drift on – if at all – as shadows. When the centre is gone, things gradually begin to fall apart.

In this sphere then we have the idea of force, of 'splendid unity', and a creative manifestation which sought to secure the stability of the nation in a just manner.

It is at this level that the Creation was held to have occurred, and the cry 'Let there be Light!' could just as well have come from the lips of Arthur whose cherished Round Table represented a veritable wheel of light spinning through the psyches of those who came for succour.

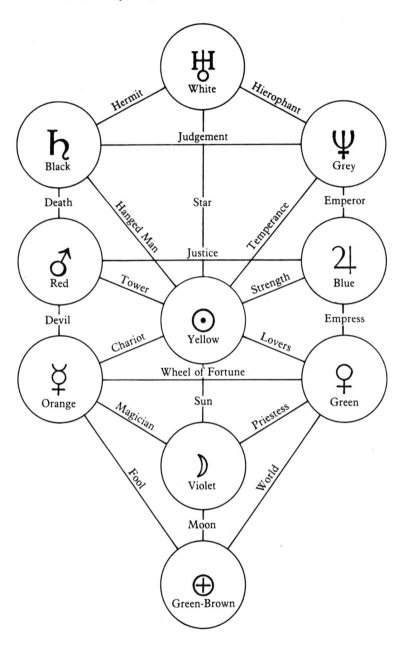

According to the magical traditions one of the qualities equated with this sphere is that of Devotion. Which of course perfectly expresses the devotion of the knights to Arthur, their king. In the early medieval period the prime loyalty for a man was not to his wife and children but to his lord. Whichever of the nobility he paid his taxes to, worked for, and depended upon, that lord was known as the 'ring-giver', and those of lesser rank were in a very binding sense wedded to him. One of the worse things that could happen was to be rejected by the 'ring-giver'. Little wonder that Lancelot, whose love for Guinevere forced him to compromise his devotion to his equally beloved King, went mad with the strain of the affair. There is an old battle chant called 'Maeldun' which expresses something of this, and the best translation is given in Henry Treece's book *Hounds of the King* :

> Thought shall be the harder, heart the keener,
> Courage the greater as our strength faileth;
> Here lies our leader in the dust of his greatness,
> Who leaves him now be damned for ever.
> We who are old now shall not leave this battle,
> But lie at his feet, in the dust, with our leader.[2]

THE EMPEROR.

Those magical groups which use the image of the Table for their inner workings tend to see it as having 13 places, all filled except for the Seige Perilous. As mentioned before, James Vogh gives us an original zodiac of 13 signs, the extra one being Arachne, the spider-goddess whose web is the universe itself. The mystical nature of the number 13 is itself derived from the lunar months in the year, the menstrual cycle, and the Mysteries of women generally. When the patriarchs set out to destroy these, their methods included proscribing 13, giving it connotations of evil, and using a zodiac of 12 signs. So, given this scheme, Arthur's table hearkens back to the primal vision of things. As far as Britain is concerned it is Rome which has to answer in large part for the attempted destruction of the feminine in Celtic society. Even so, by the time William the Bastard secured his rotten victory at Senlac in 1066, women in Britain had managed to claw back some of what they had during their Celtic hey-day. Indeed, they had more rights before the Normans came than many women have in parts of Europe even today. All in all the Roman Church has proved to be the most evil of organizations. It is only now, when its influence is on the wane, that good men are being attracted to it; the bad ones who would have become popes or bishops at least in previous eras, have reincarnated as captains of industry, or politicians. Thus when Galahad takes his perilous seat which would destroy anyone else, he lays claim to being an initiate of the Mother, he becomes the final weight needed to make the circle of Light spin without a wobble. Not surprisingly Galahad attains the Holy Grail, itself a symbol inextricably connected with the Eternal Feminine.

These two spheres with which we are concerned, the archetypal Male and Female, or Chockmah and Binah, present the interplay of what we might term 'supernal sex'. Wherever we look at the connected characters we find magical matings or wondrous births: Uther, with Merlin's help, used enchantment to sleep with Ygraine and beget Arthur; Morgan by deception and magic slept with Arthur; Elaine, by simple deception slept with Lancelot and bore Galahad. Galahad would not unite with anything but the Grail itself. Celtic parallels will follow shortly. We have already mentioned William Gray's speculation concerning the Immaculate Conception. In another book he describes, presumably by a faculty of 'far memory', an ancient rite aimed at incarnating a priest-king within the tribal group.

> Twelve active and potent males were needed, one for each
> Archetype, or Sign. They had to be as nearly perfect specimens of
> their kind as possible... one male being chosen for his wealth,
> another for his skill at hunting, another for his intelligence, and so
> on. Each was required to have some outstanding quality which alone
> would make him a worthy father, and they formed the circle of seed-
> donors or 'God-fathers'. The recipient was of course the Virgin-
> Bride...She was AIMA, the Bright Fertile One. The 'go-between'
> was a Past-Mother, Old Woman, or AMA, the Dark Sterile One.

After ritual preparations in a secluded place the men would form
the perimeter of a circle, the Maid in the centre, while the Old
Woman interweaved between the two.

> Each male...had to work themselves into a condition of
> consciousness where they were convinced they had successfully
> embodied their particular God-Aspect. This...was done by
> characteristic miming and invocations for as long as might be
> necessary...

As mistress of the ceremony the Old Woman would conduct and
guide the progress of the rite until the moment of culmination:

> It was the Old Woman who bore...the Sacred Vessel...an object of
> particular veneration. This was physically no more than a fairly
> small phallic shaped horn from some suitable animal with a pierced
> point normally kept closed during use by the Old Woman's own
> hand...The Gods were implored singly and collectively to pour their
> power into it as an instrument of doing Their Will on and in Earth.
> When the time was judged right the Old Woman of the Cup went
> deosil around the circle from one male to another collecting their
> seed as quickly as possible. They donated this not as their human
> selves, but in the character and on behalf of the God-Aspect they
> represented.
>   When the critical moment came, the Old Woman injected this
> accumulation of seed into the Maid by means of the horn which she
> blew into from the broad end, thus applying the necessary pressure.
> This was the 'breath of life' needed for the insemination process.[3]

It is a curiously touching rite, this. We can see these people on a bare plateau in Cumbria, perhaps, with snow in the hollows still, and clouds biting off the edges of the mountains around, the eternal wind scraping their bones as they gathered on that lonely spot to bring a star down into a woman's womb for the light of the tribe and their children to come. It is also a foreshadowing of the Grail vision with the mystic spear dripping into the shining bowl, as well as a prototype of the Round Table itself. It is worth remembering the esteem with which women were held by the court of Arthur. Once, in the early history of the Company, King Pellinore had failed in his duty toward a particularly distressed damsel, and this prompted Arthur to lay down the pattern of chivalry for years to come, in which womankind was to be held in the highest honour regardless of her estate.

And so we must consider now this idea of the phallus.

We have within the Eastern tradition the *kundalini*, the serpent force, which is held to be a dynamic sexual energy whose arousal results in a kind of cosmic consciousness. This 'serpent' is regarded as being coiled at the base of the spine, rising up the central channel of the spine which the tantriks call the *sushumna*. This channel is paralleled and looped around by the nerve channels known as the *ida* and *pingala*. Occult lore abounds with tales about the dangers of arousing the serpent without due preparation and understanding. Madness results, we are told, if it is not awakened properly. We find a similar tradition in Mexico with the 'plumed serpent' of Quetzalcoatl. While in the Western tradition we would call the serpent a dragon.

The transcendence achieved in raising this serpent power is almost as if the spine becomes one of the 'infinitely small straight lines' which composes the great circle of Collective Wisdom. Raising the serpent, or dragon, is akin to tapping this circuit; which is indeed a perilous undertaking, the consequences of failure resulting in a siege upon the psyche from which few could recover.

The magician's wand then, is a symbol of the spine and the serpent potential within us. And remember that in our present scheme Arthur is Pendragon, the chief or King of Dragons, an illuminated leader. When one considers the identification of Arthur with St George as convincingly given in Bob Stewart's book *Where is St George?* we take it as significant that the patron saint is always depicted as confronting the dragon with his lance.

In ancient Egypt the sceptre of Osiris was said to symbolize
power: ⅄ 'the two prongs at the lower end of the sceptre indicate
the...*ida* and *pingala*; the staff of the sceptre represents...the
sushumna.' William Thompson goes on to state that *prana* enters
the physical body from the back of the head at a point in the
medulla oblongata; while the other point in the upper cross-piece
is directed at the third eye, the pineal gland which is experienced
as being in a forward position on the brow. 'From its central
position,' says Thompson 'we can see that it is at the point that
the three brains meet.' He goes on further to note that Oedipus
met his destiny and discovered the generator of his *karma*, his
father, at the place where three roads met. The three brains
referred to are the reptilian brain of the spinal cord, which is the
brain of instinctive reflexes and the subconscious; then the limbic
ring, the brain of passion and emotion; and finally the neocortex,
the twin hemispheres of the higher mind. Talking about the
qualities needed to raise and control the serpent power he might
almost be describing the spiritual ethic of the knights in Arthur's
Company:

> One must face the subconscious, dispassionately observe the
> passions, and work with intelligence, charity and humility on the
> stones of the temple. When one has the unity of the three brains well
> in hand, then he does indeed wield the sceptre of Osiris.[4]

One can do some practical visualization with this, of the sort that
magicians call 'astral magic' or path-working.

Picture yourself entering a medieval hall which contains the
Round Table. Twelve of the thirteen seats are filled. The last one,
the Seige Perilous, is yours to claim by right. See yourself in a
simple white tunic, feel yourself to be the best knight in the
world, the culmination of our ancient heritage and yet the
precursor of a new order. You know that when you take your
proper place that a lost piece shall be found and the circle will
come alive. The other knights look at you expectantly and in
some awe. After a moment of great deliberation as to the
significance of the act you finally take your place at the table.
Arthur, at the other side, smiles at you and nods. You nod back
for this is your liege, and you have no inflated conceits. Now the
Company is made whole, now the ancient torn web is rebuilt, yet

you know that without the others you are nothing. The Company joins hands. The table is suddenly seen to be made not of wood but of light. It becomes a disk whirling at enormous speed, deosil. You can hear the rhythmic humming it makes as *awen, awen awen*...Become aware of the centre – of an invisible yet strongly felt axis. Watch the centre split open to form a hole. See the hole expand. You and the Company are now looking into the hole as it widens almost to the table's rim, so that only a thin ring of light surrounds the darkness of intersteller space. Now you can express one wish into that night but it must be as a single word. You can cry out for light, love, learning, health, unity or whatever concept is most important to you. Express this Word powerfully and imagine it travelling through the infinite depths of space. The darkness now becomes radiant, lit by stars, planets, whole galaxies which gleam like jewels on velvet, and which are the atoms of your own bones. The hole begins to close again. The surface of the Table is once more unbroken. The whole scene fades and you slowly come back to the present.

Now this is a very simple outline which should be adapted by each person as necessary. One can have six males and six females plus yourself, alternately spaced or at opposite sides. One can have all female or all male – whatever feels right. With even the slightest effort the images will tend to suggest themselves.

We can work on the physical plane too. Western Europe abounds with stone circles, standing stones and the rest. We need to make a point of choosing one and then making the effort of going to it. The very act of travelling with purpose is a magical deed which alters consciousness...

> ...for when we travel, we are jolted out of our usual routines – out of the day-to-day more or less familiar run of events that we usually live with. We are in neither one place or another; in the 'betwixt and betweens' of Keltic Mythology, in the state which anthropologists call liminality (from the Latin limen, a threshold) – a state in which doors may open to new levels of consciousness.[5]

Unless one is so inclined there is no need to perform any cosmic acts upon arrival at the chosen holy place. Presence and openness is enough for most of us. My own circle is lost within the high moors of the Borders, a world of heather and wind, black-faced sheep and curlews, and snow which clings to the shadowed places all the year round. It is a ring of twelve stones with a thirteenth outside, a very lonely place. I failed to find it on my first trip, ending up wandering on a mountainside, exhausted. On the second trip I found them lying there, long grey shapes lying askew like dead warriors. I did no more than walk from stone to stone introducing myself, giving each one gossip, touching each one. Just talking, no more. And yet, it felt as if something within me had become complete, as if the 'circle was unbroken' at last. To me it is a very powerful place. Yet now I am told that the moor in which it lies is due to be used as a nuclear dumping ground. That depressed me at first but somehow it is almost appropriate: if any place is suitable to bury fire-dragons it is there.

Not every visit need be so mundane, however. J.A. Johnston, on a visit to the Serpent Mound in Argyll wrote: 'I had a vision of a massive Serpent's head, open jaws and a cavernous throat. Although its throat was a dark tunnel it was ringed with bright points, spots of light.' To him, the throat of the Serpent was the tunnel to Truth.

Not every pilgrimage need be to near inaccessible places. Not being psychic myself, nevertheless there is a corner of a dirty back alley in Bristol which almost bowls me over, and the image of a young, near-forgotten god keeps coming to my mind. It makes no difference that this place may well be utterly lacking in any power at all to the perceptions of genuine psychics, for it is important to me. It has power for me.

We will return to the stones and sacred places at intervals throughout this book, so until then let us move with a look at the great Irish hero *Cu Chulainn*.

We get back to the Celtic tradition with this most dynamic of men, one who was so valiant, so strong, so skilled, that he could stand alone against armies. He is the chief hero of the medieval Ulster Cycle, the 'Cycle of the Knights of the Red Branch', an incarnation of dynamic and frenzied energy of such raw power that while still a youth it took the whiles of a 150 naked women to trick him into being soused in three different tubs of water before he cooled down, thus averting the destruction by fire of their city Emania. It is symbolism that will not be lost on any Qabalist.

Similar symbolism appears in the tale of his pursuit of Mider's cauldron, the latter person being a king of the underworld. Cu

Chulainn however, is a very different person to the rather dull and priggish characters of Galahad and Perceval. While those two go reverently in search of their Grail, Cu Chulainn 'the Hound' sets about stealing his Cauldron by force. In the Christian tale we have the trio of Galahad, Perceval and Bors; on the Irish side we have Cu Chulainn, Conchobar, and Curoi mac Daere. Sir Bors failed to attain the Grail because he was not completely pure; Curoi mac Daere did not get a share of the spoils because he was of a different race, namely the Tuatha De Danann. Beyond this the resemblance ends as Curoi goes on to seize all the booty for himself and insult Cu Chulainn. This naturally prompts the latter to set about recapturing the cauldron immediately, and here we find another interesting piece of magical symbolism. When he arrived at Curoi's fortress to reclaim his booty Cu Chulainn met the latter's wife, Blathnait. It was the sort of love at first sight we all dream about, for he found that he had loved her 'long before she had come from the lands of the sea...' Curoi knew that he had lost her, and drowned himself in despair. Blathnait was on the point of leaving the fortress to live with her beloved when she was struck down and killed by her husband's poet. Cu Chulainn was shattered by the loss. One significance of this is that the hero went to find his Cauldron and found the woman of his heart's desire instead. Again we see the link between Cauldron and Woman in the sphere of Saturn, showing that they are often one and the same. If Cu Chulainn had not been obsessed with regaining the Cauldron then Blathnait would not have died; but if he had not gone after it in the first place then he would never have met her, which is an indication of the sorrow Man experiences in trying to attain the Woman who is his innermost nature. It is as though, to gain something of real value, we have to give up something of equal value. D.H. Lawrence, when he was writing his great paeans to sexuality, was impotent. T.H. White yearned to have the sort of loving relationship that Lancelot had with his Jenny in his book *The Once and Future King*, but was foiled by his innate sadism which ruined all normal relationships. McGregor Mathers shared magical experiences of the very highest level with his lovely wife Moina, but their sex life was non-existent. We are tested in spheres in which we choose to specialize, and when we knock upon the doors of heaven, it is the gates of hell which always open first.

Cu Chulainn was taught his military skills by women. He was
sent to the Isle of Skye to learn under three terrible and ugly
women by the names of Dordmair, Scatach ('she who strikes fear')
and Uatach ('very terrible'). Jean Markale comments:

> Dordmair falls in love with Cu Chulainn, but he rejects her. Scatach
> offers him the 'friendship of her thighs' and Uatach becomes his
> concubine...It is clear that the women can provide their initiation
> into magic and warfare only when there are sexual relations between
> the pupil and the 'mistress' in both senses of the word.[6]

Teaching is only really effective if there is a vital interplay of
enthusiasm or energy. Again, we are at the level of supernal sex
and all magic is sexual in essence, regardless of what does or does
not occur on physical levels. The old tease that the leading man in
a play always falls in love with his leading lady is understandable,
and likewise there is always the probability of the priestess falling
in love with her priest, in magical work. Which does not always
work out for the best, and the magic inevitably suffers. In fact the
disciplines and skills of acting and magic are closely linked. Both
actors and magicians are to a great extent shape-shifters, and in
the sphere being analysed now we are concerned not just with
man but with Everyman.

Cu Chulainn of course was more than human: he had seven
toes on each foot and as many fingers on each hand; his eyes had
seven pupils apiece, each of which glittered with seven gemlike
sparkles. He had four moles on either cheek, of blue, crimson,
green and yellow. He had fifty long yellow tresses and wore a
green mantle silver-clasped upon his breast and a gold-thread
shirt. But when he was taken by his power 'he became a fearsome
and multiform and wondrous and hitherto unknown being.'
Which provides a fine magical image for working with.

As a trained man one of his first antagonists was the Queen of
Connacht, Queen Maeve, or Medb. This lady is a typical Saturn
figure, and possibly one of the prototypes of the later Guinevere.
Obsessed by power, she was wed to the simpering Ailell whose
White Bull of Connacht she greatly coveted — so much so that
she set off on a campaign to capture for her own estate the Brown
Bull of Cooley. These two bulls let it be said were no ordinary
creatures but rather representatives of the jealous gods sent by

them into Erin to cause destruction and tumult. There are hints and echoes within this tale of the ancient struggles between the matriarchy and patriarchy. Maeve's plan of conquest however, goes well until she encounters the boy Cu Chulainn who, although only 17, was more than a match for any of her champions or entire army. Just as Cu Chulainn went searching for the Cauldron and found Woman, so Maeve who went searching for the bull found Man. Robert Graves speculates that the two bulls were really royal swine-herds who had the power of changing shapes, and adds that originally, to be a swine-herd meant being a priest in the service of the Death-goddess whose sacred-beast was a pig. He also introduces a curious link between the bull and the serpent when he comments upon the alteration of women's status and contemporary myth at the time that men began to usurp the power:

> This...stage...necessitated a change in mythology. It was not enough to introduce the concept of fatherhood into the ordinary myth, as in the Orphic formula quoted by Clement of Alexandria, 'The Bull that is the Serpent's father, the Serpent that is the Bull's'. A new child was needed...[7]

He goes on to describe this being as a Thunder-child, Axe-child, or Hammer-child, who would eventually father the new Sun-god. In Mithraic terms and Celtic terms of course, the bull and the sun were synonymous. Which opens up themes that we will deal with in due course.

As might be expected, then, Cu Chulainn wreaked havoc with Maeve's army and at one marvellous moment, after countless bloody combats, we find him looking over the plain at the camp-fires of the enemy:

> At the sight a sudden anger seized him...he brandished his sword and beat on his shield until it rang with a deafening din and whirled his spear. Then opening his mouth to its widest gave forth his 'hero call'. So blood-curdling was the cry that the demons of the air, the goblins, elves and other sprites of the glen answered it and filled the air with horrible sound. Maddened by fear the Men of Erin jumped up in confusion, and in the dark grabbed their weapons, ran on each others spear-points in panic, and thrust at each other blindly, so that from panic and terror alone in the heart of the camp one hundred warriors died.[8]

This hero-call bears comparison with the Word which stirred the empty, still universe. Hero-call, victory cry, or tetragrammation, they are all similar, and have their echoes — literally — in the various 'calls' beloved of magicians. Pat Crowther, the Yorkshire witch, gives some examples of these in her book *Lid off the Cauldron*, one of the few original works on the topic. The call *aaahhi-oooo-uuuu* for example, if used by females in open space will cause males who happen to be walking past to change course and go in the direction of the call. The similar call for men to attract women she gives as: *i-ee-o-u-e-eeaie*. And there are interesting parallels here with comparable work done by William Gray in his *Ladder of Lights*.

Cu Chulainn's whole career is a distinctly magical one, and no-one could ever exhaust the levels of meaning to be found in his myth. So for lack of space we must turn now to study the peculiar manner of his death.

As might be imagined, Maeve's ultimate defeat did not lie easily on her mind and she plotted for years to kill Ulster's Hound. She was aided by a monstrous brood of ill-shapen, evil and magical creatures — three male and three female. To aid them in their task they studied black magic, finally descending to the underworld to receive from Vulcan three spears, three swords, and three knives, each one tipped with a particularly noxious venom. Curiously Vulcan seems to act with the impersonal justice of some Lord of Karma, for although he knows the weapons will kill Cu Chulainn he nevertheless holds him in high regard:

> Take these weapons and guard them well, for three kings will die by them, and one of the kings will be that king among warriors, among champions, among heroes, that king of bravery who was never yet defeated, that hard-hitting noble youth known to you as the Hound of Ulster.

These creatures set off to lure Cu Chulainn into combat by their witchery but this is spotted by his friends who prevent him confronting them. The power of the witch-brood would only last for three days and so his friends persuaded him to go to the Glen of the Deaf — a haven protected from enchantment — until the three days passed. However, sadly, by cunning methods of shape-shifting Cu Chulainn was lured into battle and refused to return to the Glen despite all the death-omens he sees en route to the fray. His priority is to the people of Ulster whom he feared to be in danger. 'Fame outlasts life, and life itself would be but a poor thing if it were bought with dishonour. For dishonoured I would be if I did not go forth now and defend Ulster against my enemies.'

He is struck with the fatal spear and death becomes inevitable. He asks leave of his enemies to go to the lakeside and quench his thirst, and they consent. Next to the lake he saw a standing pillar to which he tied himself, so that he could die on his feet like a true warrior. His blood flows into the lake; several creatures lap at it; the Hero Light dies from around his head and with the sigh of his body the stone pillar behind him splits through.

The most salient image is that of him tied to the stone pillar. Mircea Eliade describes the sacred place of every microcosm as the Centre, and says:

> The installation and consecration of the sacrifical stake constitute a rite of the Centre...the stake becomes in turn the axis connecting the three cosmic regions. Communication between Heaven and Earth becomes possible by means of this pillar. He who makes the sacrifice does, indeed, go up to heaven...upon this post now ritually transformed into the World-Axis itself.[9]

Which brings us back once more to the idea of the spine, the three brains, and the serpent force which can push us into super-consciousness. In more mundane terms the stone pillar is the phallus, the uncompromising masculinity upon which he sacrificed himself in his battles against the Queen. As the penis and its seed perpetuates a man through his children, so do the stones perpetuate a man's existence through their relative permanence within nature. Rock and stone — for all practical purposes — can stand forever as a memory to their creator: a man can live forever through his offspring, fathered from the seed within his testicles, or 'stones'.

The Glen of the Deaf is also an interesting symbol, given that the spiritual experience for Saturn, in Qabalistic terms, is Silence. We could perhaps use this as an allegory in that, if Cu Chulainn could contact the pure elements of Binah — the pristine quality of Silence in the Glen of the Deaf — then perhaps he could avoid the renegade elements expressed by the witch-brood. Basilides, the Alexandrian Gnostic who later manifested in Jung put it thus: 'It is only Ignorance, in conjunction with Silence, that can lead us down the royal road to liberation.' I like that.

Cu Chulainn is, then, another vital image we can use to vivify some of the supernal elements within us, but we must remember that he is something more than human, being more comparable to one of Dion Fortune's 'Lords of Flame and Force'. A manifestation of this figure within our psyche might be more than our placid civilized world could bear if it was not dowsed quickly.

Cu Chulainn died by a spear thrust which brought the Ulster Cycle to an end. While it was a serpent which did similar for the Arthurian Cycle, causing a knight to draw his sword during a time of parley at Camlann, the flash of light bringing forth cries of treachery and sending the hosts of Arthur and Mordred clashing. We have studied the symbols of the circle and the straight line; of the phallus and the serpent; of the dynamic male and the standing stone; of Light and Words. These are all symbols of the sphere known to Qabalists as Chockmah, which means Wisdom. If we can make our connections with these symbols in our psyches then they will point us to wisdom in our lives. We might start off as unseeing fools, but we will end as heroes.

Of course we must not restrict ourselves to the mythological images of the Round Table and the Hound alone. A very valuable and appropriate figure is that of Lugh, whose very name means 'white' and who was — is — 'Lord of the Burning Spear', this being one of the Treasures of the Irish. Any man or woman who held this in battle would never be defeated. We are told that his face 'shone like the setting sun, and he walked the earth like a god, and so famous did he become that the rainbow was called the sling of Lugh, and the Milky Way — that path of starry brightness that crosses the heavens on a frosty night — was christened the chain of Lugh.' To a great extent Cu Chulainn might be regarded as an avatar of Lugh as Krishna was an avatar of Vishnu.

And there was the Dagda too, the *Ruad Rofhessa*, or 'Red One of Great Wisdom', also known as *Eochaid Ollathair* or Eochaid the Great Father. One of the cthonic gods, he had an uncomfortable magical mating with the Morrigane, mounting her as she straddled a river with a foot on either bank.

While from the Welsh tradition there is Math, the powerful and paternal magician king.

Which is where we pause for a moment.

Although the Arthurian images fit into the pattern of the Qabalah rather well, the purely Celtic do not. Being all shape-shifters we may as well try and tie knots in a stream of water, in that as soon as the hand touches and tries to twist it into a pattern, the stream breaks into myriad gleaming drops — which still end up where gravity intended for them in the first place. If Morgan le Fay balances nicely with the Round Table it is not necessary to find a strict complement for the Morrigane in the Red Branch Knights or in any of her lovers. An Irish scholar and Qabalist might wish to do so, but it is not necessary. Even the Arthurian correspondences which form the core of this book are only given as a scheme for further thought, and should never be accepted as a new form of dogma. Crowley did the magical tradition no favours when he published his book *777*, a series of Correspondences which just do not correspond. As a collection of images for stimulating debate, yes, but as tried and tested inner linkages *777* has a lot to answer for. In the present scheme my interest is centred upon Arthur and all which surrounds him. The Celtic myths are used as sidelights to this main theme, and for myself I feel it best to leave them with their elusive, fluid qualities. Some things we cannot trap nor even try to. The different 'boxes' of the Qabalah can be useful in helping us sort out our ideas but we must never turn these boxes into coffins.

The Welsh myths, with a few exceptions, get short shrift. The Welsh culture is one which leaves me feeling blank, despite many Welsh friends. Even the sight of Wales across the Bristol Channel makes me uneasy; perhaps it is something from another life, I don't know. The loss is mine, that is certain. I know that the myths are powerful, pure and arcane, but there is just no response of the heart within me, and without this, myth and magic will not work. Welsh readers should not be offended but rather seek to do for their traditions what I cannot. Besides, if it is any comfort, I feel much the same sort of antipathy towards Trowbridge in Wiltshire, Tunbridge Wells, large portions of North America, and the entire continent of Australia.

4.

The Hawk Gods and Coming Times

Now we come to the place of Mars, the fifth planet of the Tree of Life and one which expresses: '...emotional energy, sensuality, desire to fight, pioneer, take the initiative. It is the sexual urge, energy and potency...It may convey the seeds for new beginnings...It is the masculine principle that is non-creative without its feminine counterpart.'[1] As much as any it is the planet of our times, and given the destructive potential of modern military forces perhaps our only hope is to mediate the more positive aspects of this sphere.

According to astrologers and magicians we are leaving the age of the Fishes and Dove, and entering the new one of the Water-carrier and Hawk. The obvious and over-riding fear held by us all is that of nuclear war. Not that magicians and astrologers are particularly adept at predicting any major conflicts. The Theosophical Masters gave no indication of a Great War in the offing; none of the well-known and self-proclaimed seers were much aware of the Second World War until the Stukas began to howl above Poland; while in a decade teeming with psychics and wonderworkers none of them predicted the war between Britain and Argentina over the Falkland Islands. It was Jung, with his own and his patient's dreams, who had one of the best records in anticipating such things. Long before it became politically obvious Jung was commenting publicly about the spirit of Wotan which was being unleashed in the German psyche. While it may not be possible for us to gain access to the powerful dreams of large numbers of people and draw conclusions about the future from our analyses, we do have something else: we have the dreams of our race. We have our myths. As Jung himself said: 'Everything old is a sign of something coming.' And just what that something is we will attempt to find out through the sphere of Mars.

It is the troubadors we have to thank for giving voice and word to these racial dreams. Men and women, the troubadors were more than mere singers wandering between castles, they were the vibrant expression of an attitude and emotion completely new to the times they lived in. They created within the courts of what we now know as France an atmosphere of culture and amenity toward womankind which nothing had hitherto approached, and their very songs were heavily perfumed by the Gnostic/Dualist philosophy of the Cathars whom Rome was soon to destroy. They created the mode of 'courtly love' which was gradually to alter the whole shape of Western civilization. Whether they simply expressed a current that was welling within the psyche, or whether their movement initiated that current is impossible to say. Certainly Jehan de Notredame was sufficiently impressed by them to write a history in the year 1575, some 400 years or more later, entitled *Vies des plus celebres et anciens poetes provensaux*. He also attempted some history-moulding himself when he wrote his famous prophecies under the name Nostradamus.

It is a man from this tradition, Chretien de Troyes, whom we have to consider in any analysis of the Arthurian Cycle. After all, Lancelot did not appear until 1170 when Chretien mentioned him in the list of Arthur's knights in his work *Erec*. It is he who first mentions that knight's love for Guinevere, and we first hear of the Holy Grail from him. Working apparently under the patronage of Eleanor of Aquitaine, it is Chretien who was largely responsible for laying down some images that we are still following today, like markings on a dusty road. In respect to the sphere of Mars, two of the more vital and enigmatic markings are those of *Lancelot of the Lake* and *Gawaine*.

At times, studying these figures in all the different sources, it becomes difficult to separate them. It is almost as if Gawaine is du Lac's alter ego. Chretien, for example, often uses Gawaine to make contrasts with Lancelot, as in the unfinished *Le Conte del Graal* (unfinished because Chretien was burned to death in mysterious circumstances), in which the two knights undertake parallel adventures. The difference being that Gawaine does not seek for the Grail itself but for the bleeding lance. As we shall see, this is an extraordinarily apt piece of symbolism.

Some authorities tend to dismiss Lancelot entirely as no more than an extended version of Gawaine, and point out that in some sources it is the latter who becomes Guinevere's lover, not du Lac. But there is more to it than that.

Accepting for a moment that the whole Cycle was based upon actual men and events then it is unlikely that Lancelot did exist — even assuming that Arthur, Morgan and Merlin were initiatic titles handed down through the ages. Gawaine is far more likely to have had some fleshly antecedents, his name being derived either from *Gwalchmai* or *Gwalchgwyn* which means the Hawk of May and the White Hawk respectively. Graves regards them as decidedly mystical names, while Jessie Weston advanced the theory that Gawaine was the first Grail winner.

What seems to have happened is that Gawaine, a fine knight, became regarded as a symbol of what could be achieved by martial prowess and physical strength. Lancelot, however, became expanded as a symbol to show what he could and should have achieved, not through strength alone but through power and love conjoined. Gawaine fails in the 'Queste del Saint Graal' because he relies exclusively on prowess, refuses to seek the help of divine grace and remains blind to the spiritual significance of the Grail. It is Lancelot who comes to progress spiritually further, it is Lancelot who most inspires our affections. Perhaps it is most accurate to say that du Lac was created as Gawaine's higher self. It is almost as if Lancelot were created as a symbol through which we could invoke a peculiar quality of love in the ages to come. And so let us go a step further and say that the avatar of the Aeon of Horus (according to Crowley), also termed the Age of Aquarius (the Water-carrier) will be Gawaine/Lancelot: the Hawk of May and the great du Lac.

There are indications of this back in the so-called Gnostic Gospels:

> But when the nature of mankind has been taken up and a generation of men moved by my voice comes close to me, thou [John] who hearest me now, wilt have become the same and that which is will no longer be.

This, from the apocryphal Acts of John, alludes to the tradition that at the end of our Age it will be John, the beloved disciple, who will be raised to become the next avatar. Bearing in mind the old axiom that 'all the gods are one god' then we must look for a

John-equivalent in the Arthurian Cycle. And who was more beloved of Arthur than Lancelot? The very essence of the tragedy is that this great knight loved his king beyond all men. Had this not been the case then the tales would be deprived of the poignance which gives them so much of their power. The whole life of Lancelot seems to have been a testing for the day when he would have to assume the noblest of mantles. His moral dilemma tore him apart and drove him into madness, setting him off along the path of what Joseph Campbell describes as Separation, Initiation, and Return. He became a forest-dweller, a wild-man confronting demons in the wilderness of his own psyche. If Arthur, in one of the Welsh poems, made a descent into the underworld to win a cauldron, Lancelot did much the same through his love for Guinevere. The words of his final confession as an old dying man can still wring tears in me: 'I have loved a Queen beyond compare, and I have loved her an exceedingly long time...' Confession? It is a hymn to love. If Mars, in the *Lusiad*, was regarded as the guardian power of Christianity, then Lancelot was — and is — the wish-fulfillment of the Western spirit, an incarnation of Love and Power. His is the ideal of 'muscular Christianity' which has long been advocated but rarely attained, and he has slowly reached a point whereby he might be regarded as the god-form of the new Age — a telesmic image born out of the ruins of Mordred (of whom more presently), based upon Gawaine, and deliberately created to enable consciousness to function on certain lines.

It was a mysterious mating between du Lac with Elaine (daughter of the Fisher-King) which produced Galahad, one of the two Grail winners. Although Lancelot was vouchsafed visions of the mystic Grail Ceremony he failed to achieve the ultimate of Divine Union as granted his son and Perceval. Perhaps those two youths were what W.E. Butler described as being among the 'brightest, wisest, and *meanest*' of men, as high Initiates are apt to be. They went beyond our ken while Lancelot, either through choice or lack or virtue, came back to us. In this manner he becomes a Western *boddhisattva*, who turns his back on nirvana for love of the rest of us. Who could care about the two prigs Galahad and Perceval when there is a figure like Lancelot's to aspire toward?

To appreciate him a bit more, however, we must look at his

alter-ego Gawaine in the latter's identification with Horus. According to Kenneth Grant:

> The Horus-hawk...represents the power of transcending earth. Its terrestrial shadow is symbolised by the dragon...the beast that devours the solar god...[2]

We know already that Gawaine is the Hawk of May; we read that his strength waxes before noon, wanes after it; we know about his connection with Pendragon; and we can see his connection with Lancelot when we find that the only traceable meaning for that name is from a Germanic root meaning 'land'. Further, Gawaine bore the device of a pentagram upon his shield while this same symbol is an undisputed attribution to Horus. Ares and Horus being the same word we learn that 'Aries in the zodiac also represents the Green Man, the Vernal Power of the Sun,'[3] which links us with the story of the Green Knight that is so vital to Gawaine. In ancient societies too, there was the tradition that power was passed down through the sister's son, on the principle that the purity of the blood-line was thus certain. Gawaine would

Gawaine's Star

therefore fulfill this condition as regards Arthur, being the nephew to the King on his mother's side.

His chief mystical adventure was with the aforementioned Green Knight, described in a superbly evocative alliterative poem of unknown authorship, the basic story of which is as follows:

On New Year's Day a gigantic knight appears in Arthur's court, entirely clad in green, riding a green horse. He proposes a bargain whereby any one of the king's knights may strike off his head with the axe he had brought, providing that the same knight would accept a return blow in a year's time. Gawaine takes up the challenge and is astonished to see the Green Knight pick up his head after being decapitated, order Gawaine to meet him at the Green Chapel at the stipulated time, and then gallop off with his head under his arm. The next Christmas sees Gawaine in a vast dreary forest looking for the Green Chapel. The lord of a nearby castle offers him hospitality for the remaining days before his rendezvous, telling him that the chapel in question is only a few miles distant. The lord also makes a stipulation: he will go hunting each day while Gawaine remains at the castle with his wife. At the end of each day they will exchange their spoils. While the lord is out hunting, however, his lovely wife comes into Gawaine's room and tries to seduce him. Our knight, conscious of honour and duty toward his host, will do no more than let her kiss him. When the lord came back and presented the vension he caught to Gawaine, the latter gave him a kiss — his 'spoils' for that day. The second day the same thing happened, Gawaine trading another kiss for a boar. But on the third day the lady insisted upon giving him her green, golden-hemmed girdle which this time Gawaine kept secret, exchanging a third kiss for the fox the lord had caught. The next day he set out for his appointed meeting and duly met the Green Knight next to a barrow:

> It had a hole in each end and on either side,
> And was overgrown with grass in great patches.
> All hollow it was within, only an old cavern
> Or the crevice of an ancient crag...

True to the conditions he laid his head upon the block only for the giant to take two mock blows which not unnaturally unnerved Gawaine somewhat. Steeling himself to receive the third and fatal blow he was exulted to feel the blade do no more than nick the side of his neck. Having fulfilled his promise and lived he sprang up joyfully to find that the Green Knight and recent host were one and the same, and the cut he had received at the third stroke was the punishment for concealing the girdle. The giant goes on to explain that his name is Bertilak of the High Desert, and that the lady in his castle none other than Morgan, Gawaine's aunt. Her magical powers had contrived this test:

> To put to the proof the great pride of the house,
> The reputation for high renown of the Round Table

Like a Sufi tale the true meaning of this is a secret between God and the individual interpretation of each reader; but in broad terms we can catch echoes of the head-cult common throughout Celtic society, of solar heroes, of ideas concerning growth and decay in the agricultural year, mixed with Troubador ethics concerning courtly love. From the occult standpoint however, there is the oddly fortuitous symbol of the girdle. Students of the Qabalah will know of the peculiar relationship between Mars and Venus on the Tree of Life, and in discussing the sphere of the latter planet we find William Gray commenting:

> To control Venus, the secret of her Zona, or girdle, had to be known. It was tied with a special knot, and its pattern hid the secret. Once this was mastered, Love came under control of Will, for the knot could be fastened or unfastened according to the Initiate's intention.[4]

It is Mars which gives us the strength, the will-power, to be able to exercise this control. To put it briefly, what Gawaine seems to be saying is that Love is the Law: Love under Will, which, as Gray comments, happens to be a correct teaching whether Aleister Crowley quoted it or not. It is this law which will be the basis of the times to come.

Certainly, of the two figures (Lancelot and Gawaine) it is the Hawk who is the more 'real'. His deeds seem to link with rites which go back to the most ancient days, and it is extremely significant that he is frequently referred to as 'Mary's knight'. John (the beloved disciple) becomes the protector or guardian of Mary after the crucifixion, in a similar way to Anubis becoming the guardian of Isis; while both Gawaine and Lancelot, depending upon sources, were given the task of looking after Guinevere while her king was away. So to expand a little on what we have already said the next avatar will be Lancelot/Gawaine and also John, too.

The precise nature of this 'hawk-spirit' as it manifests is difficult to determine except with hindsight – a faculty which won't be applicable for another 2,000 years in this case. Crowley however does give us some broad indications by comparing the new Aeon with the psychology of a Child.

> We may then expect the New Aeon to release mankind from its pretence of altruism, its obsession of fear and its consciousness of sin...it will suffer from spasms of transitory passion; it will be absurdly sensitive to pain and suffer from meaningless terror; it will be utterly conscienceless, cruel, helpless, affectionate and ambitious, without knowing why; it will be incapable of reason, yet at the same time intuitively aware of the truth.[5]

William Thompson argues that at puberty we experience a surge of sexual energy and awareness that makes possible the crossing of the interval between the child we have been and the person we will become, and speculates that something similar is happening to the human race as a whole.

According to Crowley the New Aeon began in 1904, and while there are strong points of comparison between his vision of the Child and Thompson's vision of the pubescent Youth the parallels are not exact. Personally I prefer the latter. One occultist expressed to me the opinion that Crowley tried to bring forward the Age in order to take the power, but for the wrong reasons, and that in any case he could not move Time itself.

While on this theme it might be pertinent to add one comment. Namely that it is easy to denigrate Crowley, because after all he set himself up more than most people. Joan Grant tells how her mother sent him slinking from the house; Gurdjieff reviled him and sent him away trembling and white-faced from the Prieuré at Fontainebleau; Henry Williamson once took a loaded pistol to Paris with the express intention of killing him; while on the other hand Dylan Thomas, the eternal child himself, was terrified of the man and so made jests about him walking on his own bath-water.

Personally I do not believe that Crowley was an Ipsissimus or even a very good magician, and am repelled and even a little frightened by some of the work of his followers. Yet it has to be admitted that on the worst day he ever had the 'Old Master', as he is sometimes mockingly called, had forgotted more about magic than I or any of my kind will every know.

We will come back to our two hawkish knights in due course, but before then we must consider another image, that of the 'renegade' aspect of Britain, namely:

Mordred

Depending upon the source, he was the child of Arthur by either Morgan or Morgause, both sisters. Whoever it was, he was both son and nephew to the king and his very birth was attended by portents. Merlin had prophesied that Arthur would be killed by a person born on May Day, the ancient feast of Beltaine, and so the king ordered all children born of nobility on the day in question to be put to death. The method of execution involved putting the babes on board a ship ('some were four weeks old, some less') and sending it out to sea. Mordred was one of these children but when the ship wrecked he became the only survivor, being washed ashore where he was found and cared for by a good man. There are obvious Biblical echoes here, and we are reminded too of Taliesin being set adrift in a coracle. If only to avenge this single heinous act Mordred aptly fits into this sphere as an implacable Lord of Justice.

There is a case to be argued, however, for Mordred having had a bad press. So for a moment let us not regard him simply as the dread figure of treachery who kidnapped Guinevere and precipitated the destruction of Camelot, but rather as the active agent of Time. There used to be an old wives' tale that a murdered man retained the reflection of his murderer upon his eyes for a few hours after death, there for all to see. Nonsense, of course (at least on physical levels) but it is as though the fatal blow Mordred struck against Logres imprinted the whole pageant of the epic upon the retina of the Western soul. And it will be a while yet before it fades to any measurable degree. The power which Mordred had, and which should have been used to develop his own kingship in due and proper course, became transmuted into the very quality which has helped preserve and intensify the feelings for the Arthurian Cycle. After all, it is human nature to love a good tragedy, and if Arthur had simply grown old and fat, dying in his bed, he would quickly have been lost to the popular imagination.

Mordred was part of the New Order of younger knights straining for recognition within Camelot. Bearing in mind that in the Qabalah Mars is called Geburah, and Saturn Binah, we can look at his function on a more esoteric level for a moment:

> Binah is called the bringer-in of death because it is the giver of form to primordial force, thus rendering it static; Geburah is called the Destroyer because the fiery Mars-force breaks down forms and destroys them. Thus we can see that Binah is perpetually binding force into form, and Geburah perpetually breaking up and destroying all forms with its disruptive energy.[6]

Which is not necessarily a bad thing, as is obvious. The act of destruction, when performed by a Sacrificial Priest, can produce energy which will 're-appear on the planes of form as an entirely different type of force to that as which it started.' So the power behind the Arthurian Cycle was transmuted, ready to appear as force of a different kind when the need arises. Perhaps it is this which is welling up in readiness for manifestation now.

If Arthur was the Once and Future King then Mordred was surely the King Who Might Have Been. Had Arthur died in the normal way then the crown would have been his by right. Or rather, the initiatic title. The fact that Mordred was conceived in a manner comparable to Galahad (and Arthur himself for that matter) indicates that he was, or should have been, another Wonderchild. We are reminded of all those individuals who have created or had created for them, Messianic mantles: there was Hitler, of course, who was once proclaimed as the 'True Holy Ghost' by his Minister for Church Affairs, and who ended his days in a bunker frothing with rages, biting on carpets, before he finally killed himself on May Eve – Walpurgis Night; there was Charles Manson who was not without insight into the darker sides of human nature but who expressed it all in a series of brutal murders, hoping to manifest his Helter Skelter vision of imminent chaos; there was Krishnamurti who was chosen by the Theosophists to become the next World Leader, the Order of the

Star in the East invoking divine energies around him only for the boy to turn his back upon the whole thing (W.E. Butler, whose own teacher was involved in this work, described how shattered that person had been when the power had failed to find its outlet); and there was Crowley himself who proclaimed himself as Logos and died as a heroin addict in a Hastings boarding house. To name but a very few.

It is the handling of power, then, which provides the acid test for those who would aspire toward kingly status on both temporal and spiritual levels.

> The right handling of power is one of the greatest tests that can be imposed on any human being. Up to this point in his progress...an initiate learns the lessons of discipline control and stability...very necessary...for unregenerate human nature, so proud in its conceit. With the grade of [Geburah] however, he must acquire the virtues of a superman and learn to wield power instead of submit to it. But even so, he is not a law unto himself, for he is the servant of the power he wields and must carry out its purposes, not serve his own.[7]

THE TOWER.

Which is a trial faced by us all on different levels: how to apply authority in a just manner within our jobs, within our families, and toward ourselves. James IV, speaking through the persona of A.J. Stewart, opined that severity consistently applied bred less discontent in the kingdom than mercy randomly administered — that from the best king any nation could have had, even if I, as an Englishman, gloated over his death at Flodden. Perhaps power is best expressed as silently and with as little fanfare as possible. Less chance, therefore, of building up the cast-iron ego which precedes the destructive current formulized by the tarot card the 'Blasted Tower'. Those magicians who loudly call themselves White are often the most dubious of all; they would be well advised to read again of Gandalf's meeting with Saruman at the Council of Elrond. It is rather like Francis of Assissi telling people in his own lifetime that he was a great Saint. Only the passing of centuries will tell if a magician was really White, or if a monk was truly saintly. Crowley, as noted, failed to handle power in the long term. Regardie felt that his former teacher's best work was done before he was 30. It might be that bringing through the Age was too much for him. Dion Fortune, many felt, suffered a similar fate. Christine Hartley saw her in her later years, a large and bloated medium, 'half man, half woman', surrounded by a crowd of female disciples, a vaguely disturbing figure. It was Christine's belief that Fortune had suffered as a result of breaking her Oath when she published some of her major works on magic.

In less exalted ways we, as students of magic, can use the technique of 'Assuming the God-form' to help mediate the more beneficent aspects of Mars, or else get them into a better balance within us. It is interesting to note that traditionally, when under psychic attack from inimical martial forces, the answer is not to invoke the opposite force (i.e., Jupiter) but to call upon the positive aspects of Mars to balance them out: Mars in its high aspects is just, never cruel; firm but not vindictive. So given that we all have a shadow-side within us that is capable of dark acts, we must find ways of creating channels which will let the darkness flow in safe, ordered directions, rather than have it flooding out in uncontrolled psychotic ways. Or metaphors to that effect.

What it involves, essentially, is assuming another identity and one which is highly specialized. On the simplest of levels an assumption of martial identity can begin with squaring the shoulders, straightening the back, holding the stomach in like a soldier on parade; mentally the magician would see himself in the very shape of Horus, or Gawaine; while emotionally he would attempt to feel within his heart the stern, strict, brave and impartial sense of Justice associated with this sphere. Other suggestive devices would be used here including the visualization and actual use of related colours, the intonation of the 'God-name', and the mental linkage with traditional figures of the same ilk. During the act of Assumption the magician, in a very real sense, becomes the god in question. He becomes something other than himself, a little bigger, more powerful, an expression of pure and concentrated energy. This is what William Gray would describe as *Being* what Thou Wilt — the expression of fundamental but neglected qualities in accordance with one's holy Will. The important addition to this however is to be able to switch off by withdrawing the supportive and suggestive symbols and returning to one's everyday self. Which will be a little bigger, a little wiser, a little more able to mediate these qualities in future. We will come back to this topic in the next chapter.

We are due for a great change, then, when the Martial forces begin to surge through our psyches. We can help to bring them through with the minimum of fuss by learning the use of their exalted God-forms. And it will be in the mystical fifth month that the Hawk God will be conceived or born. Christ after all was born on May 17 and not December 25. If coming events cast their shadows before then those shadows are getting larger and the Hawk which has been hovering in the sun for so long will soon plummet to the earth and grip us in its claws. The poet Gerard Manley Hopkins was struck by a sense of this years ago in his superb poem 'Windhover' in which he sees Christ as a falcon at dawn:

> I caught this morning morning's minion,
> kingdom of daylight's dauphin, dapple-dawn-drawn Falcon...

No-one should presume to predict the year for none of the minor annunciators have been right so far. Nor do I have access to any secret knowledge myself. Yet when I sit in my windy flat in a

Wiltshire village I can use ancient myth to anticipate holy futures, look to the night skies every May for stars which plummet to earth, and feel that past and future are the same as their opposing sides resolve, like on a Mobius strip. As the Irish seer AE once looked in every child's face for his Saviour's eyes, so might we cast around.for images of Hawks and pentagrams, and feel a little wonder that before too long they will incarnate: perhaps not in one man but in many, spreading like a psychic contagion, carrying us off on wings...

5.

The Great and Generous Queens

Behind every great man is a woman, they say. Which was a powerful and incisive comment in the years before sexual equality but a rather trite one now. While Gandhi on being asked what he thought of Western civilization, replied that he thought it would be a very good idea.

These two diverse comments become closely linked in this next sphere, which is that of Jupiter, known in the Qabalah as Chesed. Astrologically this planet relates to:

> ...religious convictions; a desire to protect, heal, preserve; ability to bring 'growth processes' to maturity, fulfilment, and to gain good fortune and favour...An afflicted Jupiter implies a tendency to exaggerate, to be extravagant, lawless, conceited, procrastinating.[1]

In the Qabalah Chesed means:

> ...not only Mercy and Compassion, but goodwill, loving kindness, and all that is associated with a Divine outpouring of unstinted providence.[2]

Further, we need only look at the traditional titles of the associated tarot cards:

4 of Wands: Perfected Work
4 of Cups: Pleasure
4 of Swords: Rest from Strife
4 of Pentacles: Earthly Power

In terms of material plenty this sphere links very closely with Western civilization, which brings us back to Gandhi's wry comment; while the woman-behind-the-man axiom sees its expression in the Arthurian image for this sphere which is none other than that of:

Guinevere

In the traditional Qabalah this is actually a masculine sphere as Geburah is feminine, but for our present purposes we must always make the Qabalah subservient to mythology, and not vice versa. Guinevere is the expression of the tarot card known as the 'Empress', and in some Celtic eyes it was she who held the real sovereignty, not Arthur. In Welsh her name is Gwenhwyfar, which means 'white shadow' — causing immediate links with one of Gawaine's mystical titles, namely Gwalchgwyn, or 'white hawk'. In *Perceval le Gallois* we find the latter summing her up thus:

> ...there has never been a lady of such renown...for, just as the wise master teaches young children, my lady the queen teaches and instructs every living being. From her flows all the good in the world, she is its source and origin. Nobody can take leave of her and go away disheartened for she knows what each person wants and the way to please each according to his desires. Nobody observes the way of rectitude or wins honour unless they have learnt to do so from my lady, or can suffer such distress that he leaves her still possessed of his grief.[3]

One magician who was working very much under Guinevere's influence, albeit unconsciously, was the actress Florence Farr whom Bernard Shaw once described as the 'New Woman'. As an Adept within the Order of the Golden Dawn she recorded this vision in 1892 in which the aforesaid Empress of the tarot spoke to her:

> I am she who fights not but is always victorious, I am that Sleeping Beauty whom men have sought; and the paths which lead to my castle are beset with danger...I am lifted up on high, and do draw men unto me...When my Secret is told, it is the Secret of the Holy Grail.[4]

In the Qabalah we find that the Magical Image for this sphere is that of a mightly crowned and throned *king*, but the relevance is still there and we can hardly separate such a queen from her king.

We must acknowledge that his throne was made secure in the first place by his marriage. And it is towards this sort of security and stability that we devote so much of our energy today – and rightly so. Chesed, and therefore Guinevere, is the upbuilding force within Nature and society. All the institutions of law and order are created through this sphere, and clearly these cannot be brought about without a stable society. Which is the significance of the throne symbol as it appears within the tarot card called The Empress as well as within the Arthurian Cycle as a whole. The achievements of Camelot could not have occurred without a stable throne. The kingship being established or ratified by marriage it went on to expand its potential by laying down a pattern of learning and a spiritual ethic. Contrasting Mars with Jupiter we can see that where Mars establishes military power, Jupiter establishes an atmosphere of learning and culture; where Mars inspires the prowess of the individual warrior, Jupiter encourages the tradition-bound cohesion of the collective.

One should remember that as late as the twentieth century custom could rule without a police force. In the *Aran Islands* J.M. Synge remarks with astonishment that when a fisherman had done wrong, he took the boat over to Galway alone to put himself in jail. Custom, the collective, and ...tradition is the force that holds [ideal societies] together. It is a question not of masculine political power, but of feminine cultural authority.[5]

If Florence Farr made an unwitting contact with Guinevere then such historical figures as Eleanor of Aquitaine and Elizabeth I of England were virtual incarnations of her spirit, for it was under their patronage that western Europe saw two outflowings of culture and development that have scarcely been matched.

The best commentary on this sphere can be found in Gray's *Ladder of Lights*:

> The greatest and most genuine benefit Jupiter can possibly give us on earth, is to fulfill our material necessities so that our minds and souls will be set free to seek nobler aims than drudging for a bare livelihood. Released from physical poverty, humans should go in search of spiritual wealth, but so many fail in this and fall victims of their own senseless greed for more and more material possessions.[6]

Elisabeth Haich, once a priestess under Ptahhotep, made the comment on a parallel theme that 'the worth of a human being begins when he is able to make a living for himself and his family.'[7]

Unfortunately — perhaps — Guinevere chose not to turn inwards once her material world was complete but outwards, to Lancelot/Gawaine. She looked to him to provide the inner light she ought to have gone looking for within herself. It is the most ancient of trials.

The atmosphere established within Camelot by its young Queen (before all the troubles, that is) was not without its drawbacks however, for we need to understand that '...even a positive change casts a shadow. We need to understand that the unique excellence of a thing is at the same time its tragic flaw.' Modern people, unable to cope with the greater amounts of leisure and luxury, unable to turn inward, are destroyed by these very benefits. Even Guinevere's love affair turned sour. Gray goes on to comment upon the very real dangers of Chesed's munificence:

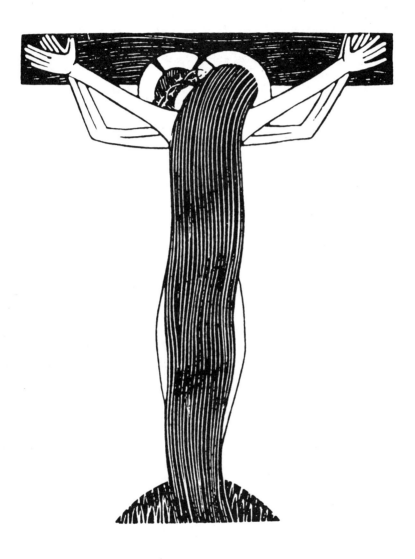

Nuptials of God (Eric Gill)

What will mankind do with their new luxuries of leisure and facilities?...Die of no more serious disease than boredom, probably the most deadly of all maladies? We have survived the experience of Geburah during two global wars, but shall we come safely through the equally challenging test of Chesed?[8]

We are faced with the challenge, then, of trying to balance the two very powerful energies of Mars and Jupiter within ourselves. Had we been straightforward creatures of only one realm, being pure expressions of only one quality, then it would be a relatively easy matter. But we are not. We are a multitude of levels and dimensions crammed into one puny frame. In Gray's system of attributions the path connecting Mars and Jupiter is allocated the tarot card known as 'Justice', and it is in the scales carried by that figure that we must look to the ideal. Jung in his *Psychology of the Unconscious* wrote that 'Where love rules, there is no will to power; and where power predominates, there love is lacking. The one is the shadow of the other.' Which has some odd reflections of some of Arthur Guirdham's interpretations of Cathar philosophy.

To come back to Guinevere then, we can see her setting the standards of womanhood, as a symbol of the kingdom's stability, and as an image of the law-giving impulse which sets any nation on its feet. Knights and even other kings *must* defer to her because they are deferring in consequence to the Law itself, to the upbuilding forces of the nation. Warren Kenton gives two valuable sidelights when he writes that anyone connected with the higher levels of this spirit is:

> ...in the least a historian, at most a great teacher founding a civilisation. This is the dimension we catch a glimpse of when we see the Acropolis or the pyramids...[9]

On mundane political levels he notes that Chesed is seen in the upper house of any parliament, for it is here that we find the elders of the tribe, the aldermen, usually past the zenith of their political ambitions and thus possessed of less biased and more generous views. He writes of the House of Lords that:

> In England this is the highest court in the land, though still beneath the authority of the Throne. Here are men and women gathered from a wide range of life...[where] archbishops argue moral points

with journalists on an equal footing...The quality of the upper chamber is greatness, and all the attributes of Hesed.[10]

We can find within the spirit of Guinevere that aspect of the White Goddess responsible for the marvellous culture of Provence, where women were something other than mere childbearers. If Guinevere was infertile on physical levels (after all neither Lancelot nor Arthur could impregnate her, while both had proved themselves elsewhere), then at other levels she was the fount of all that was best in Camelot. And we must take Camelot here to represent a state of mind as much as any earthly place.

Kenton's connection of the House of Lords to this sphere gives interesting links with a more esoteric aspect of Jupiter. Magically this exalted region is referred to as the Sphere of Masters, which is a ghastly term in any language. When a person first comes to magic he does so with the rather naïve belief that this art seeks to contact the bright spirits and High Gods and so draw the magician a little nearer the Otherworld. Later on, with much knowledge, he sees that it is a matter of contacting archetypes and personalized aspects of the collective unconscious. Later still,

with a little wisdom, he sees that he was right in the first place.

Frankly, although I like Jung, I have never *really* understood what an archetype is — though I am surrounded with all the relevant definitions even as I write. I fell into the trap, I suspect, of trying to be 'psycho-scientific' without having the intellect to support it. Guirdham, in a little booklet entitled *Beyond Jung* writes:

> What I am saying is that there is a central experience which transcends the functions and the language of the archetypes. One of its manifestations is our contact with discarnate entities...They are often a direct source of inspiration to us and the origin of much that is best in the world of art and philosophical experience. The Jungian archetypes are a fringe effect.[11]

So the real magicians have what they term their 'inner contacts', a concept which I was patronizingly sceptical about during my 'psycho-logical' days but which I accept now. Although I must affirm once more that I have made nothing approaching an inner contact myself.

Dr Guirdham then, has his Cathar entities Bertrand Marty and Braida de Montserver to link with inwardly; one of Dion Fortune's contacts had once walked the earth as a certain L. E. who had been incarnate under one of the Georges; Crowley had his Aiwass; Jung his Philemon; while Christine Hartley had contacts with F.P.D. many times after his death in 1943, and judging from people I have spoken to of late she is not the only one. The old mage certainly spread his wings a lot once he got to the Otherworld. These contacts might be entities for whom one felt affection in his life or a previous one; they might also be very ancient and powerful entities indeed, as hinted at by the titles of the various Golden Dawn temples: Isis-Urania, Hermanubis, Amon-Ra. How 'pure' the contact is, how faithfully the energies or ideas are transmitted, is a matter of perpetual dispute among the occult fraternity and is something beyond our scope here.

It is through an inner contact therefore, that the magician brings something across from the Otherworld. Dion Fortune describes this through the mouthpiece of her character Vivien le Fay Morgan in her excellent novel *Moon Magic*:

That which I did then, in those hours of intense power and emotion, up there in the darkness of the moon-temple with the river in flood outside, went into the group mind of the race to work like leaven...There is freedom in the world today because of what I did that night, for it opened the first tiny rift in the great barrier and the forces began to move chanelling and eroding as they flowed, till presently the strength of the waters came flooding through like the bursting of a dam and all resistance melted away.[12]

Deliberately or not the magician provokes a change within the consciousness of the group, the nation, and ultimately the world. People who do pioneering work in the arts and sciences are as involved in opening the Moon Gate as any magician. Although it is often the case that they need do no more than operate the lock, for the pressure behind each Gate is invariably so great that it flings itself open when the lock is undone. The torments of artists such as Van Gogh and Cezanne are well known, and their achievements assured that mankind would find a new way of looking as things. Jung described the immense pressure and the parapsychological phenomena which built up within his house before he wrote that odd document *Septem Sermones ad Mortuos*. He said:

As soon as I took up the pen, the whole ghostly assemblage evaporated. The room quieted and the atmosphere cleared. The haunting was over.

Gareth Knight, referring to this Sphere of Masters describes those entities as 'human beings who have gained all the experience, and all the wisdom resulting from experience, necessary for their spiritual evolution in the worlds of form. They are thus "just men made perfect"...' who elect to assert a guiding influence upon our civilization.

Although it has been said that judging from the results so far they seem just as prone to errors as ourselves. Gandhi's comment at the beginning of this chapter is not so very far off the mark. Perhaps it really is the case that there is a perpetual War in the heavens between Light and Dark. In Guinevere's case it could be argued that it was the Darkness which eventually triumphed.

While on this theme we might mention the particular vices that the Qabalah associates with this sphere, namely: Bigotry,

Hypocrisy, Gluttony and Tyranny. These are clear indications of what results when these expansive forces get unbalanced. Too much law-giving becomes tyranny; too much luxury produces gluttony; too much in the way of self-conscious niceness and do-gooding can produce bigotry and hypocrisy. The weakest and most ineffective people I have met have been aspiring magicians or earnest social workers. Which reminds us of the old axiom that unbalanced Mercy is Weakness. To Lancelot in the depth of his despair there could not have seemed a bigger hypocrite or tyrant than his Queen when her jealousy over Elaine caused her to condemn him. And her tyranny in the name of love was notorious, causing her to command her lover to lose joust after joust in a tournament until his debasement satisfied her.

We will pursue this White Shadow a little more in the section on Arthur, but until then we might consider:

Etain

With this woman we are given a god-form that we can use for magical purposes. The fullest description of her is to be found in the old saga 'The Destruction of Da Derga's Hostel'.

> He saw a woman at the edge of a well, and she had a silver comb with gold ornament. She was washing in a silver basin on which were four birds of gold and bright little gems of purple carbuncle on the chasing of the basin. She wore a purple cloak of good fleece, held with silver brooches chased with gold, and a smock of green silk with gold embroidery. There were wonderful ornaments of animal design in gold and silver on her breast and shoulders. The sun shone upon her, so that the men saw the gold gleaming in the sunshine against the green silk. There were two golden tresses on her head plaited in four with a ball at the end of every lock. The colour of her hair was like the flower of the iris in summer or like pure gold after it has been polished. She was undoing her hair to wash it, so that her arms were out from beneath her dress. White as snow of one night were her hands, and her lovely cheeks were soft and even, red as the mountain foxglove. Her eyebrows were as black as the beetle's back. Her teeth were like a shower of pearls. Her eyes were as blue as the Hyacinth, her lips as red as Parthian leather. High, smooth, soft and white were her shoulders, clear white her long fingers. Her hands were long, white as the foam of a wave was her side, long and slender, soft as wool. Her thighs were warm and smooth and white; her knees small and round and hard and bright. Her shins were short and bright and

straight. Her heels were even and lovely. The blushing light of the moon was in her noble face a lofty pride in her smooth brow. The radiance of love was in her eyes; the flush of pleasure on her cheeks, now red as a calf's blood and changing again to snowy whiteness. There was a gentle dignity in her voice. Her step was firm and graceful. She had the walk of a Queen. She was the fairest, loveliest, finest that men's eyes had seen of all the women of the world. They thought she was of the fairies. Of her it was said: 'All are lovely till compared with Etain. All are fair till compared with Etain.'[13]

In the traditional Qabalah the following symbols are associated with Chesed:

Colours: Deep violet; blue; deep purple; deep azure, flecked gold
Titles: Love, Majesty
Number: 4
Symbols: Orb, Equi-armed Cross, Throne, Sceptre, Crook
Spiritual Experience: Vision of Love
Virtue: Obedience

In her book *First Steps in Ritual* Dolores Ashcroft-Nowicki hints at an operation of High Magic along Egyptian lines in which the priest uses his own anima in place of an actual priestess, energizing the Star Centre and entering into psychic contact with the Goddess. She gives due warning that this is not a trivial act and one not to be attempted by the profane and unwary. But human nature is such that if the nerve is there the act will be attempted anyway, no matter how inexperienced the student. So if an image of the anima is to be created with a view to eventual extrusion then we can do worse than use that of Etain. She is in fact an image of Majesty in its highest sense, the Majesty of Love.

Christine Hartley avers that the story of Mider and Etain is the original of that of Arthur, Mordred and Guinevere: 'Mider, the King of the Underworld stealing the Queen from the sun, and we are standing once again on the threshold of that eternal combat of the Light and the Darkness for the Spring time...'

The actual details of this romance can be found in any library, as there is no space to recount it here. The object of this book is to provoke the reader into using myth to create his own inner connections, and this can only be done through sheer hard work.

The study of magic, like acting, is 99 per cent perspiration and 1 per cent inspiration. In one of his essays FPD enjoined the student to ask himself before retiring to bed: Has my brow been wet this day with mental sweat? Which is a very sound injunction despite the air of Victoriana about it. Gurdjieff put it another way when he said, 'All energy spent on conscious work is an investment; that spent mechanically is lost forever.' The wand of a traditional ritualist is imbued with a very real power by virtue of the effort gone into making it, as well as all the related concepts of time, space, matter and energy with which it links. The images of Mider and Etain, therefore, as well as Gawaine and Guinevere, are no less real than any piece of physical impedimenta within a ritualist's temple. It could be argued that the impact of technological stimulii such as television has caused the new generations of minds to respond more readily to such internal fantasy. It is as though the cusp of the Piscean Age with the Aquarian Age has brought us to the crossing-point of the Mobius strip, where we find ourselves moving onto the other loop and inexplicably over into the Otherworld.

What we might try to do is to anticipate how this Guinevere-aspect of present society will be modified by the appearance of her Hawk God. Bearing in mind the speculations of the last chapter Gray's analysis of the tarot card the 'Empress' is worth looking at:

> ...the Empress represents what used to be called quite plainly 'good breeding'. Otherwise intentional production of high quality humans. Once people were either 'well' or 'ill' bred. This depended upon genetic characteristics being carefully chosen and related. Originally it had nothing to do with money or social status, but was meant to indicate facilities for incarnation among advanced souls capable of leading others...They became what was later termed the 'ruling Classes' but unhappily history has shown up their failures rather than emphasised their successes. They did not fail quite as badly as many nowadays might like to suppose. Despite everything they managed to get something of their evolutionary characteristics into humanity.[14]

While Elisabeth Haich prophecies that in the Aquarian Age (which is also influenced by the complementary sign of Leo) 'dominion will be concentrated in individual persons – dictators – who group the people about themselves and guide them. In this epoch people discover traffic and intercourse with other planets.'

In a way, consciousness will slowly begin to function along what might be termed tantric directions. The old troubadors introduced what was at very least a coy form of tantrism into the West, the romantic expression of which was in the complex modes of Courtly Love. Colin Wilson in his novel *The God of the Labyrinth* speculated on the idea that if the moment of climax could be sustained and controlled then it could enable consciousness to break through to the Other side. Perhaps we are at the brink of a cosmic conception in which the once-sterile Guinevere is about to be quickened by her lover, the spiritual climax of the act carrying the consciousness of humanity across into the New Age. Whether we can make this transit without war is the crucial question. Kenneth Grant writes:

> But the idea of Mars being a god of war and *bloodshed* is merely a derivation from the primary one of shedding blood in *conception* for the first time. Thus, 'with the Egyptians, Mars was the *primeval generative principle*.'[15]

Pray to the Gods that those magicians who are busy invoking at these levels of Power and Majesty know what they are doing. Two global wars this century are surely enough.

While the last word must be left to William Thompson whose writings stimulated this line of enquiry in the first place, rather than those overtly occult writers quoted alongside him:

> Once it was physical death and crucifixion which nailed consciousness down into matter; then it was a sacrament of Thanatos; but in the world-epoch about to begin it is a sacrament of Eros, a physical sexuality in which the lovers of eternity give birth to the world on the physical plane. The avatars of the New Age...will not be solitary male, but the male and female together.[16]

6.

The Unconquered Sun

The original draft of this book was written during one winter of unemployment seven years ago now. Those were iron days, huddling next to a one-bar electric fire and feeling the cold snap like a guillotine more than a yard beyond its radiance. Even the sun seemed to fail me that winter, dribbling weakly through the window and sliding over the floor as thin oil. As the time dragged by it became harder to concentrate on the discipline of writing. I reminded myself of the magical maxim that every event, every obstacle, and every delight is but a mysterious dealing between the individual spirit and the spirit of God. But sometimes in trying to see this my mind failed to make conjunction with my eyeballs, and in between the flicker, the blink and then the darkness, there was only cold, emptiness, and the bare wall behind the typewriter.

And yet during those weeks preceding the Winter solstice I knew that while the whole northern hemisphere including Bath, England, was tilted away from the sun, yet the earth itself was actually nearer the sun than during the Summer months, due to some law of cosmic harmony. So, following the maxim I could tell myself that although my own axis of opportunity apparently pointed toward nothingness in those days, an inner sun was nevertheless close to me, unseen, ready to swing into view and warmth in good time.

Plus it was Samhain when I started the book, the old Celtic festival which marked the earth's swing into darkness, when the world must necessarily lie stripped and bare and scoured to the bones for a while. So I should have expected some hardship without whining about it.

The innermost core of the book, of course, was Arthur. He was the hidden sun that was near me and towards which my own axis would slowly begin to point as I progressed in my orbit.

In the Qabalah we can see that there is a central sphere which holds the whole pattern together. This is known as Tiphereth, which means Beauty or Harmony, and its astrological association is with the sun. In the same way Arthur is the central link for the whole of his myth system. Without him there would be no Camelot, no Round Table, no questing for the Holy Grail. He was the centre. He is our centre. As Yeats' famous poem put it, if that centre should fall apart, then 'mere anarchy' would be loosed upon the world. When the sun dies, we die.

Arthur is the strong central figure then, the one who holds the group together and resolves their antagonisms. Although as noted in the section on Power there is usually a limit to how long such a person can cope before the schisms start. It happened to the Theosophists and it happened within the Golden Dawn. Samuel Liddel Mathers who created the latter was originally described by Yeats as like a 'walking flame'. Many years later he became 'half lunatic, half knave'. Instead of remaining like the sun he became a Black Hole, collapsed within himself.

In the Egyptian traditions the sun was regarded as the Eye of

THE SUN .

God looking down upon humanity. What individual solar figures become is the Eye of the people they guide. An Eskimo shaman described what it felt like after his own spontaneous initiation into those mysteries:

> ...I was a shaman. I could see and hear in a totally different way. I had gained my enlightenment, the shaman's light of brain and body, and this in such a manner that it was not only I who could see through the darkness of life, but the same bright light also shone out from me, imperceptible to human beings but visible to all spirits of earth and sky and sea, and these now came to me to become my helping spirits.[1]

It is this inward radiance which draws people in the first place and then holds them. It is this, more than the philosophies, which is important.

In the old text of the *Sepher Yetzirah* we find that this solar sphere of Tiphereth is called the Mediating Intelligence, which was precisely the role of Arthur as a good and effective king: he mediated between the disputes of his knights; he balanced the rivalries; he held his knights in check as the sun does the planets. In the Tree-glyph this sphere is the equilibrium of Mars and Jupiter; in other terms, Arthur was the balance between Guinevere and Lancelot in that both loved him and for a long time both were held to him.

'Arthur' as we have said, was probably an initiatic title. It seems to derive from artos, or bear, which would have been one of the totem creatures of the ancient societies. In the rites of Mithras there were seven grades: Raven, Bridegroom, Soldier, Lion, Persian, Courier of the Sun, Father. We can easily make the extension from this to imagine a pre Roman system in which the Bear and Hawk were prominent.

Though we must not, like modern magicians, get overly glamoured by the concept of grades. A vital quality of Arthur was that he expressed Everyman, or the concept known to Qabalists as Adam Kadmon. Arthur is the sun, and it was from the sun that all the planets of our system were originally flung. In the Qabalah this is known as the sphere of harmony and perfect balance, which superficially at least tends to create associations with Arthur along the 'gentle Jesus meek and mild' lines. Which could not be further from the truth. The sun is a sphere of harmony only in that its colossal and violent energies are kept in control. It is a perfect balance of lethal opposites. Only someone as strong as Artos the Bear could manage the different pulls exerted by the Round Table given him by Guinevere's father. So this solar sphere, placed as it is between the columns of positive and negative should not be regarded as '*neither* strict *nor* relaxed' but as both.

There are three traditional Magical Images assigned to this sphere which are as descriptive as the devices on each knight's coat of arms.

First, the image of the Child.

Arthur was something special. A wonderchild. One of those deliberately incarnated by the various rites hinted at in previous chapters. Arthur Guirdham states in his book *The Great Heresy* that when the male is taken over in benign possession by discarnate entities during the sexual act, the offspring will be a great hero, or leader. When the female is taken over thus the child will become a seer, or prophet. We might see something of this in the conception of Arthur, when Uther Pendragon availed himself of Merlin's shape-shifting spells to sleep with Ygraine, who thought it was her own husband. After his birth it was Merlin again who spirited him away to be raised by the kindly Sir Ector, in the Forest Sauvage. The latter being a fine symbol for the unconscious. Merlin the Magus of course was fully aware that an important entity had incarnated. He became Arthur's tutor just as the Lake Lady became the instructress of Lancelot. In Tibet the Dalai Lama was reputed to give his priests signs before his death as to where he would reincarnate, while F.P.D. told Christine Hartley that his next incarnation would be as a Chinese doctor. (As a matter of speculation I believe that I have already met him, as a little Chinese boy living in a happy house in a large American town.) Quite apart from anything esoteric there is also the idea of the Child as symbolic of a quality of soul. The sense of being child-like but by no means childish, with a wisdom expressed by openness and charm. One of the Huxley's said that we must learn to sit down before Fact like a little child, which is an attitude we might apply to the study of magic too. In a sense this Child-ideal as it is seen within adults can only be attained after one has a full range of human experience. Many of the great lechers in history, and some of the more bizarre sects such as Rasputin's Khlysty, aimed at the concept of purity and innocence through satiation.

The second Magical Image is that of a Majestic King, or rather a Priest-King.

It is in the latter that we have temporal and spiritual power united. In occult history we see this within the *Winged Pharoahs* or illuminated rulers described in Joan Grant's excellent novel of far memory. Just as the solar sphere seems equidistant between heaven and earth, so did Arthur mediate between the worlds. After the vision of the Holy Grail at Pentecost the knights had made their own inner contacts, to use magical parlance, and went their own ways. Which is the whole point of magical training in the first place.

Thus there are essentially two types of magical group: those which function on a level of amateur philosophy, discourse, and ritual dramatics – all of which appeal to the intellectual levels. And those which have made a genuine inner contact appealing at very gut levels. Usually the latter degenerates into the former, rarely the other way around. It is the solar energy at the centre of each system which is important and which keeps it alive, not the analyses of planetary orbits. Arthur, Artos, Ar-tur, was the wonderchild, born to be king and blessed of the Gods; the best and brightest in the world were drawn to him.

The third traditional Image is that of the Sacrificed God.

All commentators on mythology have noted the frequency with which the concept of the Sacrificed God is encountered. They invariably tend to be solar figures or with solar connections of a strong kind. Christ, Osiris, Dionysus, Balder, and then Arthur. All were sacrificed for the love they had shown their peoples. In *The Rollright Ritual* William Gray makes some valuable comments about the psychology behind this idea. He shows how, as tribal society began to need a strong central ruler to unite and direct the various factions, so they also needed a means to ensure that such a ruler would never over-reach himself.

> The fact remains that if one of the Kings were periodically and ceremonially slain in the presence of all his people, this sacrifice had a profound effect upon their entire attitudes to life...The sight of a Ruler being reduced to a mass of flesh and blood no different from anyone else's carved-up carcase was a very sobering spectacle indeed.

To see the highest and mightiest in the land solemnly brought down to the lowest common denominator...was an emotional and psyche-altering experience of the deepest significance. There was a communal feeling of empathic equality with the new-killed King, which became superseded by a sense of surviving superiority. Especially if the ceremony was concluded by a shareout of meat and drink provided by the flesh and blood of the martyred monarch.[2]

The important aspect of this act was that it was entirely voluntary, the compensations before death being power, privilege, wealth and esteem for the duration of what would otherwise be a very short and hard life. In some traditions the actual killing was performed by what Graves calls the tanist, more popularly known as the Dark Twin. This was, in some sense, the king's brother – the incarnation of the bright king's own shadow. In Marion Campbell's excellent if badly flawed novel of that name the Dark Twin was the dreamer, the prophet, the introvert, while the king was his very opposite. Between them they encompass all the qualities needed to protect and illuminate the tribe. At the end of a certain period of time deduced from the stars the king would be murdered by his brother and the new king take his place. Michael Harrison in his book *The Roots of Witchcraft* gives solid support to Margaret Murray's statements concerning the Divine King in England, in which this ritual murder of the monarch was said to continue until Plantagenet times. It sounds to us rather a gruesome concept, but we must note that consciousness once functioned very differently to the way it does now. It is said too that the Aztecs who had the most gruesome of state religions were the gentlest of people; while we who have the gentlest of religions in Christianity are the most savage of all.

But there is another side to the Sacrificed God image, and that is the idea that the god will eventually resurrect. In most of the tales Arthur is not exactly dead but rather sleeping, awaiting the time when Britain will need him again. This is not so very different from the concept of the Resurrection, of both Osiris and Christ. Leaders or gods which have an especially plangent appeal are rarely allowed to fade away. We need them too much. In tribal societies the old kings were held to be on the Otherside but still very close to the tribe and functioning on its behalf. Reincarnation was to be within the tribe. In this sense the favourite kings would surely come back to them again. In a different and contemporary way there was a brief but popular rumour that John F. Kennedy had not died by the assasin's bullet but was severely incapacitated, ready to be wheeled out to inspire the nation at moments of peril. Some fans of Walt Disney insisted that the latter's body was preserved in ice until the time when scientists could unfreeze him and bring him back to life with advanced technology. Four and a half centuries before that the Scots whispered that James IV had not died at Flodden but had found the Philosopher's Stone and thus the secret of eternal life. The Duke of Marlborough was held to reincarnated in his own descendant Winston Churchill. The possibilities are endless, while the hope and the need for such a thing will last for as long as the sun rises from our nights.

Child, Priest-King and Sacrificed God: three images exquisitely suited to the figure of Arthur even if they did originate within a country and tradition far removed from Camelot. Supporting these is the so-called spiritual Virtue assigned to the sphere of Tiphereth, which is that of Devotion to the Great Work. Dion Fortune writes:

> Devotion might be defined as love for something higher than ourselves; something that evokes our idealism; which, while we despair of becoming equal to it, yet makes us aspire to become like it...When a stronger emotional content is infused into devotion and it becomes adoration, it carries us across the great gulf fixed between the tangible and the intangible, and enables us to apprehend things that eye hath not seen, nor ear heard...[3]

Above all the sun is the sphere of Vision. And if there are problems associated with handling the power of Mars, with utilizing the bounty of Jupiter, then there are as many decisions to be made when opening the Vision of the Sun. Merlin was said to have burst out laughing when he came across a beggar at his wits end and lamenting his fate, because his vision showed him that the man was sitting upon a buried treasure trove. Likewise the sight of a happy man made him weep because he foresaw disaster for that wretch's family. In Trevor Ravenscroft's *The Spear of Destiny* we read how that great, though dull, mystic Rudolf Steiner became aware through his supernormal vision of a forthcoming attempt on his life. Yet he took no avoiding action as he believed that such visions should not be used to dodge the events of everyday life. At the last moment however, one of his followers who had learned of the plot through normal means came to warn him, and only then did Steiner feel justified in taking avoiding action. If cruelty is one of the negative sides of Mars then pride is one of the downfalls for solar consciousness and vision. The Dublin eccentric Desmond Kavanagh held that his country was the 'Isle of Fire' mentioned in Egyptian texts – that place of light beyond the limits of the world, where the gods were born or revived, and whence sent into the world. In his last months he became so identified with the images of the Phoenix and Sun that he agonized obsessively as to cause and effect: did he simply forsee events? or did his visualization actually *cause* them? For his wife it became the last straw when, as a stray shaft of light illuminated their bedroom one morning, his eyes took on their glazed look and he asked: 'Is it the sun — or is it me?' He died under a tropical sun by an act of self-immolation at Heliopolis. His wife had always maintained he was a lousy seer, anyway.

The type of vision equated with this sphere is something other than psychism in the usual sense of the word. Rather should we describe it as the quality of intuition, or inspiration, which D.H. Lawrence described as 'the intelligence which arises out of sex and beauty.' Einstein had a radiant flash of intuition in which he determined his theory of Relativity before his intellect was able to ratify it. It is as though our normal consciousness was periodically affected by solar flares which ram out into the darkness like priests' fingers of light. There is an occult tradition that ancient consciousness functioned very differently indeed, the sense of Otherness being more pronounced, clairvoyance accepted as fact. In *The Celtic Realms* we find the passage:

> Clairvoyance is widely recognized and its incidence is usually preceded by the verb *adciu* 'see' – ie with my eye of inner vision...The technique for obtaining a supernatural vision is recorded verbatim in one Irish text and is known as *Imbas forosnai*, 'Inspiration which enlightens'.[4]

Bearing in mind what we have already said about the Lunar and Solar epochs we can find interesting parallels (though not direct equations) in the speculations of Dr Julian Jaynes. In his book *The Origin of Consciousness in the Breakdown of the Bicameral Mind* he states that as recently as three thousand years ago our ancestors functioned primarily through the right half of the brain — which in simple terms is responsible for what we might call psychism in the broadest sense. The left half of the brain, in contrast, provides intellectual processes, vigilance, cruelty, egotism, nervous tension and a penchant for study and progress — in short the qualities we most associate with Western man today.

Clearly the ideal would be for the two halves to function with equal facility without one being largely subordinate to the other. The magician Dolores Ashcroft-Nowicki feels that the answer to this is to be found within the limbic ring, the mid-brain. Which is perhaps the place where 'the three roads meet' as mentioned in an earlier chapter. To her this limbic ring is the rainbow bridge between heaven and earth known to the Norsemen as Bifröst. Somehow we have to learn where this bridge is and the right passwords to enable us to cross and return at will.

Having completed the above I came back from my work recently to find that the postman had left a large padded envelope on my doorstep. When I opened it it could have been a shower of stars which fell out, my wonder was so great. Inside was a bundle of notes, sent from Christine Hartley, which record a series of magical workings for the years 1937-38, involving herself, 'Kim' Seymour, and on several occasions the redoubtable Dion Fortune.

On opening the hand-written pages at random I came across what follows, which was so obviously synchronistic that it demands inclusion. Although each participant in the workings wrote up his or her own experiences separately for the purpose of cross-checking, it is Seymour's account which I reproduce here.

Friday, 25.3.38. 8.30 to 11 p.m. Moon on last Quarter. Self fit but very fed up with the Belfry Isis Rite.

1. Built up the Magical Personality, then built the Tree in colours. Then woke the 7 Centres and built them as coloured lotuses. Finally placed the Egyptian gods on their lotus (note this time Har-Par-Krat came up first on Tiphareth next Herakhti). Then we stood up visualising the White and Black pillars and cross linking the centres, and calling down both the powers of the Pillars ran them through the Magical Personality.

2. Placing hands on each others' shoulders we used the M.P. and grew to an immense size and floated high above the Earth. Suddenly I saw an immense rainbow which became Bifröst, and over which we floated looking down into an unfathomable depth, between two cliffs of black rock, which was Nifl-heim and the abode of the giant in flames.

And as we crossed we saw Odin the All-Father waiting for us. He was smiling and not terrible as he was the last time we saw him. He was, one felt, the god of universal Wisdom. His image was dark clad, a dark cloud about his head, and one eye was bandaged; his two ravens Hugin (thought) and Munin (memory) were perched on his shoulders.

Below his feet were the two wolves Geri and Freki and behind him was Valhalla. He offered C.C.T. [Christine Hartley] three gifts which she might ask for. First she asked for courage and he said you already have it. Then she asked for Judgement and he said you have it already if only you will stop to think. C.C.T. delayed over the third boon and he said Wait, you can ask again when in real need.

Then we saw the Gods Balder, Freya and others. But we were pushed back across Bifröst, and looking down I saw the tree Yggdrasil and below it in the roots the dark forms of evil and destruction.

Suddenly we were back.

It was vivid and powerful, and this symbolism was intensely real, and C.C.T. was rather shaken. She slept a few moments while I got tea.

After tea we decided to sit and see what came, for the last vision came as we were standing working the Tree...

Christine's own visions support these but are recorded with much less detail. After brief refreshment they resumed the working and made the powerful Egyptian contact for which they had originally aimed, Seymour ending this particular account with the rather touching words: 'Then we came back very tired and pleased. Something new seems to have come to me — a sense of confidence and a reality in the work that now lies before me'.

I have heard this self-doubt uttered by all the real magicians that I know, and it is something which, for me, enhances their integrity. Dion Fortune expresses it well in her novel *Moon Magic*:

There are times in every magical operation when I ask myself if I am self-deluded – am I really what I think I am? This is due to the discrepancy between the two modes of consciousness – the normal brain consciousness, and the higher consciousness that includes subconsciousness and transcends it, for it contains memories not only of this life, but of all past lives and all their knowledge. In trance work we disconnect the normal consciousness and use ultra-consciousness only; in magic we use both modes of consciousness simultaneously. We have to use the psychological analogue of double de-clutching, and inevitably there is a loss of power as the gears disengage and re-engage. It is at that moment that the horrible doubts and fears come in. They pass again as the power comes through and the magic picks up speed, but they are bad moments while they last.[5]

I would add that in considering this magical record of Christine's in its entirety this unsought-for Nordic excursion looks to be the least satisfactory. But on reflection I am inclined to think that this single rite has been 'working like leaven' ever since, and is perhaps the one which will most surely affect the rest of us today...

7.

Merlin and the Magicians

When Christine and Kim sat in that room at Queensborough Terrace, assumed their Magical Personalities, and took that inward trip across the rainbow bridge they were taking with them the thin gleaming thread of Western consciousness. Because of that working, in ways that they might never have dreamed, it has become less difficult for us to follow.

Not all of us, however, belong to functioning units of priest and priestess, and to reach this limbic ring or rainbow bridge across the gulf which separates us from the Otherworld, we need a guide. The Egyptians had Thoth, and also Anubis who was the Opener of the Way. Here in the West we have Merlin.

In the system we are using now he would equate nicely with Mercury, whose urges are:

> ...to communicate knowledge, facts, and to teach, in terms of the *mental* processes and intellect. Mercury is unemotional. Thus Mercury shows the ability to consciously interpret all that is continually passing through the brain.[1]

We could say that he is the left brain, the thinker and teacher and 'cunning man', the master-architect of Stonehenge. He is the lord of the Hermetic Path, by which is meant the whole body of ritually applied ideas which go to form modern magic. We can see a fine god-form of him in the tarot card called 'The Magician'. He is the Initiator of the British Mysteries and one of his graves is to be found where a tributary joins the Tweed, which knowledgeable fishers know to be a salmon-rich river. He is known in those northern parts by the mystic name of Lailoken; in other places he is Myrddin. He has always been the 'little bird' which tells us secrets.

As the Initiator he leads the aspirant toward the Mysteries; while in another sense it was he who started (initiated) these Mysteries in the first place. In other words the *hierosgamos* he arranged between Uther and Ygraine resulted in the expected Wonderchild, and began the whole cycle. Those people who favour the bicameral theories can make much of that.

To a certain degree Merlin has been smothered by generations of story-tellers who have cast him and his magic into rather a decrepit frame. Which is somewhat unfortunate as the disciplines of ritual magic require strength and vitality. Arthur Guirdham noted that psychics are invariably stout or heavily-built people, often downright fat owing to the slower metabolism – and not at all of the willowy kinds found in popular fiction. Hartley writes:

> Merlin is not the rather cantankerous old magician of some of the more modern versions, growing angry, losing his temper and waving his staff in the air; properly interpreted these are all part of the work of the magician in forming his magic; they are the outward symbols of the power of the magus; the fully directed force of the power of concentration behind him.[2]

If there is a modern development that this magus would appreciate it is the system of the Qabalah. It has been described in bombastic terms as the 'mighty all embracing glyph of the Universe and the soul of man', but the exasperating thing is that it really *is* that. It functions at such an appalling level of veracity and flexibility that the pattern of the Tree fits into the unconscious like liver in the body: cut it, and it grows again. Students of Hermetic magic devote regular exercises to building the symbol into their aura. Once they have done that then it will endure throughout their lives. Sometimes I wish I had never heard of the system.

The original version of this book went into immense detail, restating every minute aspect of the Qabalah in Celtic terms. The traditional intra-sphere subtleties were expounded at length and it all fitted together splendidly. Looking back it was the most tedious thing I have ever written. Nowadays I try to wither into my roots, as Yeats would say, and the older I get the less I know. So those who are new to the Qabalah must take much of this on trust and accept that I am erring on the side of simplicity.

Which leads us into the statement that the realm of Mercury, known in the Qabalah as Hod (pronounced *hood*, meaning Splendour, or Glory) is profoundly linked with Chockmah. And if this Arthurian speculation is to prove valid than we must find strong relationships between Merlin and the Round Table.

The mage did, of course, play his part in both arranging Arthur's marriage and securing the Table as a dowry. More, by his magic, he caused the names of the forthcoming knights to appear in gold letters at the appropriate seat. Not only is he the Initiator then, he is also the Interpreter. The Vision of Splendour is there before him, he shows the right way to the right people. He is Mercury/Hermes, one of the Messenger-gods, ensuring adequate communication from one land to the other, taking us from our chintzy worlds toward the Gate of Moon itself. Gray extends this a little more when he writes:

Besides being a Messenger, Hermes was the patron of all secret dealings, acted as a Guide of the dead to the Otherworld, was a good-luck bringer, and a God of roadways...Hermes Trismegistus [Thoth] was the Thrice-Great instructor of the Secret Wisdom...[3]

THE MAGICIAN.

These are the aspects of Merlin too: the messenger, the secret dealer, the guide and teacher. Yet despite all these qualities we rarely see him to the fore in any of the Arthurian tales. He acts, and then retires happily into the shadows like his former pupil Morgan. In one account we find him telling his biographer, Blaise, to write down some details about his birth:

> The Apostles write nothing concerning Our Lord that they have not seen or heard for themselves; thou too must write nothing about me but what thou hast heard from me. And because I am dark and always will be, let the book also be dark and mysterious in those places where I will not show myself.

Here we find the age-old injunction of the magician to Know, Will, Dare, and above all Be Silent. It is the latter Merlin refers to: there are some things which should not, and indeed cannot, be spoken of. It is a silence born not of perversity but necessity. There are levels of consciousness which cannot be described via the processes of the left brain. Even Crowley when he claimed to have become an Ipsissimus did no more than make a matter-of-fact statement in his Magical Diary.

WHEEL of FORTUNE.

We might now summarize Merlin's career in the light of the left-hand pillar of the Tree.

First of all we note his connection with the birth and coronation of Arthur. Through these he is connected with a particular Level of Fate, or even causal action. This is the level expressed by the tarot card 'The Wheel of Fortune' connecting Hod and Netzach. The birth and coronation were both uncertain times; like fixing a weight on the top of a wheel, we wonder which way the wheel will turn, clockwise or anti-clockwise. These events were moments of a crucial importance but uncertain direction. Merlin the Initiator began them, the rest was up to God.

Later on in his life we learn that he goes mad with suffering (as did Lancelot) and hides himself away in the forest from fellow-men. This suggests, surely, the card known as the 'Hermit', connecting Binah (or Sorrow) with Kether.

His actual dwelling place within the forest was a tower (The Blasted Tower?), where he devotes himself to astronomical observations, explores the stars, and sings about future happenings. Within the latter activities we can see the card 'The Chariot' linking Mercury with the Sun, or Intellect with

THE HERMIT.

Intuition. In a sense this card expresses the nature of magic. Lao Tzu put it thus:

> The further one goes, the less one knows.
> Therefore the sage knows without going about,
> Understands without seeing,
> And accomplishes without any action.

It is T.S. Eliot spending his days in the basement of a bank and his nights writing poetry which would turn the whole genre upside-down. It is Neitzche doing not very much at all on outward levels yet writing books which would inspire dark and often hideous impulses. It is Sitting Bull predicting the future of his tribe while Custer's men shot themselves to death at Little Big Horn. They didn't move, but they travelled further than anyone.

At the foot of Merlin's tower issued forth a spring of crystal clear water from which a wandering madman drank and became cured. We can see in this wretch the Fool which is the first and the last card of the Major Arcana, for Merlin counselled the now-sane man to go on and find God who 'gave thee back to thyself'.

The mage's occult knowledge was such that it gave him the loneliness that only the visionary can know (the Hermit again), especially so since some regarded him as a devil, which is the card linking Mercury and Mars. While finally, when he has taught all that he can he retreats into 'eternal silence' and vanishes into a rock tomb aptly symbolized by the card 'Death'.

Having established his credentials what we must now consider is his connection with the Sword in the Stone and with the Lady of the Lake.

Even today the arcane symbolism of the sword has vital importance in ceremonial magic. It is a physical symbol of one of the tools or 'weapons' used by the magician to forge his way inwards. The other weapons are: the wand, shield, and cup – all of which can be seen in the tarot card 'The Magician'. In the quaternary circle of the Elements it associates with the east, with Air, with thinking, logic, aggression and quickness. Unlike the other instruments on the magician's table the sword is the only one which specifically needs a high level of concrete thought to create the shape, cutting edges, grip – quite apart from the qualities needed to fashion the material of the weapon in the first place. The cup, staff and shield can be made with comparative ease, but the sword-maker is an intellectual, a thinker, a proto-scientist who can tease the iron from the earth and shape it to his will. It is interesting to compare Merlin with the various Celtic smith-gods of the early Bronze and Iron Age cultures, for the workers of metal had real eminence within the tribal societies.

> The Celtic smith is almost invariably an arcane figure with uncanny associations, a wizard capable of making supernatural weapons, an idea that may have descended from the time when metals were novel elements and appeared to possess supernatural attributes of sharpness and life-taking quality.[4]

These gods of smithcraft, although providing kings with the power to win empires, were rarely warriors themselves. The supreme importance of the smith was that he gave a man a means by which to extend himself, either through the snob value of owning an expensive weapon, or, literally, by increasing his reach and potency in combat.

It is fitting therefore that Merlin's role in making Arthur king is so tied up with the Sword in the Stone, the withdrawal of which could only be effected by some quality other than sheer brute strength. The sword itself is a symbol of wisdom: whosoever could draw wisdom from the stone must necessarily *have* wisdom. Merlin, it must be emphasized, does not own the sword in question (in fact some sources say that Gawaine is the real owner) but he does lead Arthur to the sword. In this act he is again the Initiator bringing the candidate to the Gate of Moon and arming him for the battles he might enjoin on the Other side.

The famed Excalibur is in fact a separate sword to the one pulled from stone, and again it was Merlin who led Arthur to the lake where a samite-clothed arm appears holding both sword and scabbard aloft. When Arthur took Excalibur from the Lake Lady his tutor asked him which he prized most, the sword or scabbard. The young king chose the former and was then upbraided by Merlin, who told him how valuable the scabbard was: while he wore it no drop of blood would be lost. Bearing in mind the obvious phallic symbolism involved, there is a case to be made here for the idea that it was descent through the female blood-line which was held to be most royal.

Mythology is full of examples of heroes who own magical swords given them by magicians or smith-gods. Manannan had three swords known as 'The Retaliator', 'The Great Fury' and 'The Little Fury'. Nuada possessed a mystic sword from Finias; Finn owned a similar weapon named Macan Luin; Rhydderch Hael owned the sword Dyrnwyn. But it is only within the Arthurian Cycle that the sword is balanced by its counterpart of the scabbard. As we shall see very shortly this is of great significance within our present scheme. But before then we must consider the unusual image of:

The Fisher King

This unusual figure was – and is – the guardian of the Holy Grail. He is often known as the Rich Fisher. His British name is King Pelles, while his continental equivalent is Amfortas. Both have the same description and serve the same function, being old sick kings agonizing from a wound in the thigh and unable to hand over authority until the perfect Grail-knight comes and asks a certain question. When this is done the wound heals miraculously, the Wasteland of his court flowers, and a new cycle begins. In his role as Guardian of the Grail we can see that the Rich Fisher is closely linked with Merlin, who stands at the door of the Mysteries, the Gate of Moon. The landscape of the Rich Fisher's realm is that seen beyond the pylons in the card known as 'The Moon'. His daughter is Elaine. His grandson is Galahad.

All of which leads us to suspect something odd. In many ancient literatures and oral traditions the genealogies were given prominence. The titles and roles of the present characters are so charged with hidden significance that they become like Zen *koans*, ostensibly meaningless questions or statements which can yet cause consciousness to explode with enlightenment when the enigma is unravelled — and every man achieving this with a different solution to the same thing. We are faced with something of the sort now. If the questing Knight had to ask Pelles the meaning of the holy processions in the Grail Castle in order to revitalize the Wasteland, then there are several Grail Questions that we might ask ourselves:

What is the relationship between the Knight of the Lake (Lancelot) and Pelles, the Fisher King?

What is the significance of Elaine's *hierosgamos* with the unwitting du Lac?

In giving birth to the mystic Galahad did Elaine in some way replace the sterile 'white shadow' that was Guinevere?

Is Elaine, daughter of Pelles, to be connected with the Elaine who was the sister-queen of Morgan and Morgause?

Each man must fish around for these answers within himself, after asking Merlin for help. Whatever answer he can pull out from his depths is the right answer — for himself. The Wasteland within his psyche will slowly begin to flower again.

Marie-Louise Franz makes the following observation:

Curiously enough, another saga motif...was joined to the legend of the Grail vessel as early as the Middle Ages: the figure of Merlin. In several French versions of the Grail saga Perceval, in his search for the Grail, keeps coming across the tracks of a mysterious being who is finally revealed as the 'real secret of the Grail'. It is Merlin...Perceval soon meets him as a man with a wooden leg, as an old man with two snakes wound around his throat, as a grey-haired hermit clad in white like a spirit...[5]

Strangely enough this image of the man with a wooden leg is strongly suggestive of the Fisher King with the wound in his thigh; the two snakes are those on the caduceus possessed by Mercury; and the hermit is very much Merlin in his old age.

Franz then goes on to connect Merlin with the secret of the Grail itself, and mentions Jung's summation of the whole question: 'Seek the Self within, and then you will find both the secret of the Grail and the answer to the spiritual problem of our cultural tradition.'

One of the things to note is that the Rich Fisher was wounded in the thigh — which is usually a euphemism for the genitals, the wound in question often going as far as ritual castration as found in some of the more extreme of ancient cults. Assuming this to be the case then Pelles/Amfortas is at one level a symbol of Fallen Man. This is an echo of the Gnostic heresy that we do not really belong on this world at all, that our race is 'of the starry heavens', and that we have become divided creatures lost within matter. Which is why the Grail Question is so important: as soon as we ask the reason Why? then the Merlin-ic elements within us begin to lead us on the long journey back to our true and fertile home 'beyond the moon'. The act of castration can thus be seen as a crude attempt to make the Rich Fisher – paradoxically – a more complete person, man and woman conjoined. And it is this which takes us back by slow degrees to the scabbard and sword symbolism of male/female, and onto another odd and prophetic image within this bastard Qabalah of mine. Namely, the

Hermaphrodite

In one of their magical workings aimed at Ishtar, Seymour makes the following note: 'A queer thing happened, a sort of egg of faint light built around us and enclosed us so that we became two halves of one whole.' Which of course is an expression of the old injunction that to find God, one must first find the Man within the Woman, and the Woman within the Man. Magicians invariably specialize at some time in working with a particular partner. Crowley had a succession of Scarlet Women to act as his *shakti*; Lawrence had his Frieda; while Dion Fortune's husband was the M.O.H. for Amersham, one Dr Penry Evans whom Christine described as a very powerful magician indeed, better than his wife. In the ancient of days F.P.D. had been a priest of Ptah and C.C.T. a priestess of Sekhmet who had had the marks of

THE HIEROPHANT

Thoth stamped into their auras and enjoined to act through the ages as a functioning unit.

It is in such examples that we encounter the two-becoming-one concept. As much as anything else magic is the quest for Wholeness. During rites of the sort described the participants become, for brief if timeless moments, 'At One' with something greater than themselves.

What we must do, though, is discard the image of the hermaphrodite and replace it with the rather more subtle and revealing one of the androgyne. Which takes us back to the prophetic words of William Thompson who wrote: 'The avatars of the New Age...will not be solitary male, but the male and female together.'

It is interesting to note that shamans of many tribal cultures have deliberately cross-dressed to achieve this androgynous appearance.

The shaman's attire makes him appear to be neither man nor woman, but rather a living metaphor for his mediating role as a highly respected healer who stands between man and the spirit world. In this case cross-dressing is more a ritual than a psychological act, the uniform goes with the job.[6]

Nor does this necessarily imply effeminacy or homosexuality, for the cross-dressing shamans not only have wives and children, but often several mistresses too.

Crowley went to great lengths to describe his own androgyny, including the developed breasts, and in carnal terms he was a fully bi-sexual person. Naturally he projected his own qualities as foreshadowing the New Aeon and commented about the latter's onset: 'Observe for yourselves...the strange modifications of the reproductive instinct with a tendency to become bi-sexual or epicene...'

Dion Fortune was described as 'part man, part woman', something she was naturally aware of. Rupert Malcolm, the character in *Moon Magic* describes his Lilith Le Fay with the words: '...and yet she is not wholly feminine by any manner of means. There is something curiously male about her.'

Which brings us back to the New Age again, whose currents were deliberately invoked and anticipated by the magicians already mentioned. Grant writes:

> The hawk of Horus resumes in a single symbol the concepts of height and depth, North and South, female and male, heaven and earth.[7]

We might pose ourselves another Grail question: What is the connection between the hawk of Horus and the merlin attributed in the sport of falconry to ladies?

As each person creates his god-form of Merlin to function in the inner worlds, so must he answer that question for himself. Which is another way of saying that I really don't know.

What seems fairly certain however is that very gradually an androgynous strain will make itself known during the next two millenia. Quite apart from the magical scene we can see an anticipation of this within the colourful if bizarre musicians who sprang up in the 70s, notably the mercurial David Bowie during his 'Ziggy Stardust and the Spiders from Mars' days.

While as a sideline to this we might look afresh at the mental disorder known as schizophrenia:

> The psychiatrists, after years of vainly attempting to determine the
> cause of schizophrenia, turned the problem over to the biologists. In
> the laboratories...spiders fed on flies which in turn had been fed on
> plasma from the bloodstreams of schizophrenic humans, ceased to
> spin their orderly webs and began, suddenly, to spin loose, shapeless
> webs. Other spiders, fed on the blood plasma of victims of other
> types of mental disorders, continued to spin their orderly trim
> masterpieces.[8]

Which has tended to convince biologists that this split in the
mind is caused by some foreign substance within the blood. In the
book *Operators and Things*, which is a remarkable account of a
journey through schizophrenia, Barbara O'Brien quotes one of
the more extreme theories: ' "I am convinced" said one biologist
"that the schizophrenic is an attempt on the part of nature at
forming a mutation." ' She goes on to add that the number of
humans now being born with the capacity for developing strange
chemicals in the blood is a startling phenomenon. 'The biologist
who threw up his hands and said, "It is mutation" at least has
statistics on his side.' Although it is not a theory she is
particularly convinced by she feels it is worth more than a casual
dismissal. Indeed it is.

> Is man now in the process of adapting to an environment too
> complex or too restricted for his present physical or mental
> equipment? Is he in the process of becoming something capable of
> dealing with an environment which is, itself, only beginning to shape
> and which the force of life is sensing? The first attempts at creating
> birds probably produced creatures which looked like poorly adapted
> lizards...I shall prepare man for a changing universe, says the river of
> life, so that he may be able to live in it. In the process of
> experimenting to develop new man, I shall make more than one
> mistake. The first birds were failures but in creating the failures, I
> learned finally to conquer air.[9]

It was once thought by millions that Hitler was the New Man. It
is said that at a point early in his rise to the level of dictator a
woman psychic screamed at him that he could still choose
between the White and the Black Magic, that his course was not

inevitably toward the left-hand path. There is something disturbing in the fact that of the seven children conceived by his mother Klara, four died prematurely, one was moronic, and another was hidden from public view as an idiot. It sounds as if the Merlin-ic forces behind Nature tried again and again to shape the type of man they wanted; but even Merlin can make mistakes. Perhaps because of failures like the schizophrenics, psychopaths, and all those Crowleyan/Hitlerian channels who burned themselves out through the handling of power and the shaping of worlds, the androgyne strains will start to appear with more surety and success.

8.

Venus and the Lake Ladies

It was at Brean Down that I almost saw her — the Sea Priestess I mean. I was on a holiday then with a group of Down's Syndrome children. It was a period when flared jeans and long, lank hair were de rigueur, while studied nonchalance was the air to cultivate. It had been a long trip and we were all tired, but a strong breeze broke the tops off the waves, whipped the sand into flying devils, and kept us all in the bus watching the grey sea beneath the dark sky. Something reminded me of the scene in Dion Fortune's lovely novel *The Sea Priestess* when the young and fragile Maxwell first sees the latter in a dream:

> And as they drifted past within a stone's throw, I saw, sitting high in the stern poop, a woman in a carven chair. She had a great book in her lap...and I saw she had a pale face and scarlet lips, and long dark hair like seaweed in the tide. Round her hair, binding it, was a gold and jewelled band. For those few moments as the boat wore off the sand-bank I looked into her face, and she into mine; and her eyes were strange eyes, as of a sea goddess.[1]

Brean Down was indeed the original setting for this novel. Miss Morgan's temple can be seen in the old ruined fort, and there is one particularly atmospheric cave just where it ought to be. It should be remembered that there was once a Golden Dawn temple at Weston-super-Mare, along the coast, while Dion Fortune lived and practised magic at the foot of Glastonbury Tor, in chalets now owned by Geoffrey Ashe, the Arthurian scholar.

So she floated into my mind that day, the Sea Priestess did, as I sat there on the threshold of earth and ocean, beneath the grim sky, giving out sandwiches to a group of children not wholly in the world themselves.

THE HIGH PRIESTESS

And she came to Arthur Waite and Pamela Colman Smith too, who got her image down in the second tarot card of the Major Arcana. Along with the Hermit, this is my favourite card.

She guards what is traditionally known as the Orphic Path, and is the sensual, erotic, aspect of the Empress. I have glimpsed those sea goddess eyes of hers so many times, but every time I thought I had finally claimed her she was gone, like a broken reflection in a pool. It is Merlin and she who attract people to magic in the first place, he being the lord of the Hermetic path, she, Vivienne, being the lady of the Orphic. And people come to them, for the most part, not out of high spiritual ideals and the relentless search for Truth, but simply because they are lonely, and feel inadequate. The great magicians — the *real* magicians — are born and not made. The rest of us have to use them as models, accumulating *mana* along the way until the life comes when we can incarnate with our own supply of Light. It is a hankering back to Gurdjieff's idea that man has no soul, only a potential; and that the way to fulfill this potential is through inner work and suffering. It is a hard statement but a true one; and if anyone is likely to give us our soul it is the Lady. The lonely ones go straight to her, the ones seeking power look toward Merlin. Later on it is seen that both are necessary. Without the Master Therion, Leah Hirsig would have been a nonentity, living a life so flat she could have seen her own tombstone at the end of it. But with him she was the Whore of Babalon, and Time itself gestated in her womb. While as a nervous and lonely boy in a Northern mining town I could sit in my bedroom looking out over the colliery rows and pit-heaps and whisper out the haunting words: 'I am a child of Earth, but my race is of the starry heavens'; as well as Levi's: 'I have omnipotence at my command, and eternity at my disposal.' Magic kept me sane.

On a more collective level it was the fertility cult now popularly called witchcraft which provided a palliative to the miseries of medieval life. Their gatherings were occasions for joy, feasting, and procreation. Michael Harrison has done some brilliant work in translating what had hitherto been regarded as nonsensical chants within the rites of witchcraft. What he has proved is that these chants are in the Basque tongue and refer to the simple pleasures of a ceremonial feast. Which delightfully explodes the notions that such phrases as 'Eko Eko Azarak; Eko Zomelak' are expressions of a sonic science harking back to the Atlantean days.

The Orphic path is also known by the nicer term of Green Ray. The method of the Green Ray is to impinge upon the unconscious through the emotions. Merlin does likewise but through the intellect. Needless to say the range of emotions released by Green Ray workings can vary from intense lust to the frenzy of the Bacchantes who would tear living flesh apart with their bare and maddened hands. On a more sedate astrological level we are dealing with the planet of Venus which handles

> ...the power behind loving, need for affection, desire for the beautiful, the artistic, aesthetic...It is the feeling within the creative impulse: the essence of creativity. It is not the physical aspect of sex: it is the desire to unite opposites, to re-create the image of oneself in one's opposite, and of the opposites in oneself.

The fertile delights of this Ray have never been especially prominent within orthodox Christianity — which has been described as a Sterility Cult. Instead of a wise witch using the girdle of Venus to harness our emotions, we have had to submit to

THE LOVERS.

the Mother Church using an iron corset. Although for once this organisation is not as much to blame as some might aver. It was not so much the moral strictures of Rome or Canterbury which defeated the Old Religion: quite simply it was the pox which did it. The Churches merely jumped upon the death-cart as it trundled along. From the fifteenth century onward the pox began to spread across Europe with increasing speed. Nothing was more likely to lessen enthusiasm for promiscuity than syphilis. It also coincided with two developing trends: a lessening of the fatalism common to early societies which was once expressed by the saying: 'the wyrd goes ever as it must'. Needless to say, when fatalism weakens, people become more acutely protective of their health. While the second trend was the destruction of the mutually supportive rural communities throughout the advent of the Machine Age. It was harder to support an illegitimate child in an impersonal city. A previous pestilence, bubonic plague, had already weakened peoples' respect and fear of an appallingly corrupt Church. The eventual reforms of the Catholic church and the birth of the Protesting churches coincided with the time that fear of syphilis reached its height. It was only then that Rome and Canterbury really managed to assert a moral control over the people. So except for a short period in recent centuries, and only thinly spread, England at least has never been a truly Christian country. Swami Omananda put it more succinctly, describing the English as the race of greatest natural mystics in the world. As far as physical disease curbing magico-religious tendencies goes, we might see a parallel today in which the promiscuous Vivienne aspects of modern society are thinking twice, faced by the threat of Herpes Simplex II. Unless Merlin can bring his science to bear in good time then we might see a return to a new form of puritan ethic.

And now from a general view of her nature let us look more closely at this dream-woman, this

Lady of the Lake

Even in exoteric mythology and folk-lore there are indications that Morgan ('born of the sea') and the Lake Lady are one, though on different levels. In terms of the Qabalah it is interesting to note the connection between the 'Great Sea' and the 'Bitter Sea' to use the titles of Binah, and the lake at Netzach, its lower analogue. Nimue, or Vivienne, will eventually develop from a Lake Lady into a true Sea Priestess, and supporting this we have only to look at Botticelli's Venus being born from the sea to gain some workable image.

In simple terms what we are taught by the Lady is that through passion and romance do we learn about Understanding and Sorrow. In a materially secure Western world nothing will lead us to understanding (via sorrow) more surely than love. There is a tale from Wales called the Legend of Llyn y Fan which expresses something of this.

> There was once a young man who herded cattle next to the shores of Lake Fan. One day he noticed on its waters the most enchanting young girl, and he quickly fell in love with her. Gradually, he plucked up the courage to talk to her and even met her father, who lived under the surface. The old man told him that he could marry his daughter on the condition that he did not lay hand on her three times without reason. As a dowry, the youth was given a herd of cattle. After some years however, he quite unintentionally touched his wife for the third time without reason. Lamenting, she disappeared under the waters, taking the herd with her. She came back only once to see her children.[3]

This indicates the very nature of Venus, and the Lady. As Dion Fortune writes: 'In Netzach force is still relatively free-moving, being bound only into exceedingly fluidic and ever-shifting shapes...' Just as this fairy bride — actually called the Lady of the Lake — has but a tenuous connection with the overworld, so is passion destroyed by any attempt to chain it. May as well try to keep a candle alight within a sealed bottle. Folk-lore is rife with accounts of marriages between fairies and humans, and although Stan Gooch regards this as a folk-memory of the times when Cro-Magnon mated with Neanderthal, in the mythological sense the message is that unless the humans concerned forsake the overworld life then such marriages are doomed. It is a case of stay or go; and either way you lose something.

In the tarot card of the High Priestess we see her sitting before a veil. Behind that veil we can catch a glimpse of waters. In life, once we step through the illusions we project onto our lovers we find ourselves in out of our depths with the knowledge that we must sink or swim. There is another story on this theme which we can look at, describing how:

> Gwestin of Gwestiniog was returning one night after some revels when he heard some fairy folk talking in a pond near Brecknock Mere. He learned from them – without them knowing he was listening – how to constrain and marry a particular creature who had taken his fancy. When he sprung his knowledge upon her she agreed to marry him and swore fealty until such time as he struck her with his bridle-rein. She kept to her word but of course one day the inevitable happened and Gwestin struck her in such a manner. Immediately she fled back to her home in the pond as Gwestin tried to stop her, and with difficulty he managed to retain one child.[4]

Of course Gwestin could hardly have expected anything else. If we demand constant passion or love from any being momentarily possessing a Vivienne image, then we might get more than we expect. But more probably nothing at all.

Algernon Blackwood, a novelist who studied magic in the Golden Dawn, was obsessed with this theme of love 'beyond the Looking Glass'. In very quiet and different ways, we all are. The world of Vivienne is best seen with the innocent passion of a child, when Tir na'n Og is discovered and explored in the clouds of a rosy sunset. It is most beautifully and profoundly expressed in the diary of the six year old Opal Whiteley which caused such a controversy when it was first published in 1920. The odd and precocious child of a lumberman in Oregon, one of her journal entries reads:

> As I did go along, I saw many grey rocks. Some grey rocks had grey and green patches on them. Some of these patches had ruffles all round their edges. The grey patches on the grey rocks are lichens. My Angel Father said so. Lichen folk talk in grey tones. And the things they say are their thoughts about the gladness of a winter day. I put my ear close to the rocks and I listen. That is how I do hear what they are saying. Then I do take a reed for a flute. I climb on a stump – on the most high stump that is near. I pipe on the flute to the wind what the lichens are saying. I am piper for the lichens that dwell on the grey rocks, and the lichens that cling to the trees grown old.[5]

She never knew it, but she was a Piper at the Gates of Dawn. If I had that six year old's vision and writing talent now (instead of lifting my imagery without acknowledgement from obscure sources) then I would cross my arms upon my chest, say the *nunc dimittis* and await the end with real contentment.

However, as Christine Hartley comments:

> ...it is not wise for the student or the tyro to venture out of his own element into that faery land; before he can travel safely in so foreign a country he must learn the way to return, or he will find himself drifting helplessly forever in the twilight, neither admitted beyond the fairy portals nor able to return to take up his earth life. That is the land of Illusion, which the student of the mysteries must learn to recognise and pass through on his way to the true Moon country.[6]

It was her teacher and co-worker F.P.D. (whose bones and shewstone from a previous life can be seen in Wells Museum) who gave the best solo workings yet published, entitled *The Old Religion*. Adapting just one of the many exercises given in that article then the reader, if female, must utilize the triangle of Morgan, Arthur and Merlin; if male, then he will work with the images of Merlin, Vivienne, and Morgan.

Use this green triangle as follows. If you have a trinity of two gods and a goddess, place the goddess at the apex. If two goddesses and a male god, then place him at the apex...Visualise the apex of each triangle as touching the altar...a double cube about four and a half feet high. On it is the sacred light. You as priest or priestess stand at the altar facing east. Before you, dimly seen in the darkness of the Sanctuary in the East, are the conventional forms of the three gods, or goddesses, or the mixed trinity you decide to use. Behind you are the two priests or two priestesses of the gods or goddesses that form the basal angles of the triangle.

Build that scene until it appears automatically the moment you are seated for your meditation...

You may get a surprise the first time you try this method. But in all probability (as happened to the author) you will get nothing without many weeks of steady concentrated visualising with strong desire.[7]

It is indeed a powerful exercise, and although it should ideally be worked with the aid of two others actually sitting behind you to form a physical triangle and assist in the creation of the Divine triangle at the Other side, it can be worked alone also. The mind just has to exercise itself over a broader area, visualizing and *feeling* both the priestly triangle and the godly triangle it mirrors.

This of course is old knowledge indeed to Merlin himself. His own contact with the Lady of the Lake resulted in his being shut up in a cave. Or a tree. Or a tomb — depending on which Merlin it is. Basically the story is as follows:

Merlin met a young girl called Vivienne, whose father was Dyonas, which means 'god-son of Diana, goddess of the woods'. Merlin fell in love with Dyonas' daughter, but Vivienne would not accept his love unless the secrets of his magic power were revealed to her. Merlin knew what would happen if he did this, but he carried out her wishes anyway. Finally when he was sleeping one day in the Forest of Broceliande, Vivienne cast a spell on him, and he found himself a prisoner in an enchanted castle, but happy with the young woman he loved.[8]

This Gallic version (more optimistic than the British) contains valuable imagery. First of all Vivienne is connected with the mysterious forest of Broceliande. 'The forest...is one of the universal images of femininity' writes Jean Markale; 'It is in that forest that the Submerged Princess awaits her lover.' It also takes us back to the Green Ray Workings which can lead mere humans so much astray. Second, it is she who entraps him, in the most desirable of ways. The other way around and it would have been disastrous. As it is Merlin yields, through love, and he becomes prisoner in the sense that a butterfly can imprison us when it lands on our shoulders: we are enchanted, we keep still, we watch from the corner of our eye.

Malory's version is essentially the same except that Nimue gets so tired of Merlin's sexual overtures that she traps him in a cave and leaves him. Which is a less than pleasant ending to an idyllic start.

Of course we can avoid such a thing happening to us. All we have to do is avoid any contact with which ever sex enlarges our emotions, adopt an attitude of strict detachment, and blinker ourselves against anything but the goal ahead. Yet if we do that we fall victim to the dismal aspects of the Piscean Age: we become cold fish. I was an acned youth the first time I fell in love and got jilted. I blamed it on magic; I was afraid of the alienation that this study would bring; I recalled something I had read or mis-read by Alice Bailey saying that women were the downfall of most great mystics. It seemed to me then that she must be right, for after all she had occult visions, she had handled Cosmic Fire, and what had *I* ever done but get one more 'O' level than Prince Charles? In despair I wrote to a well-known magician famed for his irascibility but who had always been very kind and straight with me through the medium of letters. He replied as only he could: 'Balls to Alice Bailey the pompous old prude! All these so-called "Great Mystics" make such a hopeless muck of their own lovelives it's just laughable. I wouldn't take their views too seriously if I were you.' That casual and earthy comment set something free within me in ways that divine philosophies never could. Regardless of what she might do to us, we would be fools to reject what the Lake Lady can offer.

Another way of looking at it is that:

Vivien can be taken as the symbol of the new form of belief which was coming in; each new dispensation means the dispersing of the power of the former one.

Vivien is young and Merlin is old; she shuts him up and destroys

THE WORLD.

his power; her name stands for life and living and vitality; she is the strength of the new age.

When Merlin yields to Vivien his work is done, and it matters little whether he is incarcerated in a rock or in a fairy hill or whether he disappears into his glass house, for the intention is the same.[9]

The thrill of Vivien can be felt when falling in love either with a person, a place, an impulse, or just the sheer magic of a particular moment. She gives new life, just as Chockmah at the top of the pillar promotes life in the first place.

Remember that the sphere of Netzach is a sphere of dynamism while Hod is one of restraint. If there is no Netzach influence to introduce a dynamic element, the over-preponderance of Hod will lead to all theory and no practice in occult matters. To an extent this has already happened. We have de-glamourised magic, we have tried to explain it too much. The Romantic poets used to curse Newton for explaining the rainbow, and they about got it right.

Although the irony here is that Newton himself, possibly the greatest mind of all time in terms of left-brain functioning, was a deep and confirmed mystic but one whose mystical premises are almost embarrassing to read. Likewise there are mystics around with real vision, real power and authority who yet show abysmal deficiencies in more mundane areas. Which gives more credence to the metaphor that the connection between the left and right hand brains is not so much the Rainbow Bridge (which after all is but a segment of a circle) but a Mobius strip. Newton went so far back into the left brain that he circled under and entered the right brain from the lower levels – but getting twisted in the process.

That is just a metaphor however; make of it what you will.

Having said that we must now climb on Merlin's back for a little while and look at the Lady's place upon the Tree. As noted, there is a connection between her and Morgan le Fay, at Binah; her connection with Merlin at Hod is obvious; and it was she who gave Arthur his sword at the beginning and who took it back at the end. There is also a very profound connection with the Hawk Gods in the sphere of Mars which we will deal with now.

Fortune wrote: 'We shall observe at once that the symbolism contains two distinct ideas – the idea of power and the idea of beauty; and we are reminded of the love that existed between Venus and Mars according to the old myth.' We have already mentioned the image of the *zona*, or girdle, as per Gawaine, and I have recently been told that one of the secrets of Rennes-le-Chateau is the pattern made by the orbit or *zone* of Venus around the sun, it making a five pointed star. While for our present purposes it is fortuitous to find a definite link between Lancelot and the Lady of the Lake. In *Lancelot en prose* we read how King Ban fled with his wife and child from his enemies, and headed for the court of Arthur. Upon climbing a hill in the forest of Broceliande he turned to see his fortress aflame behind him. The shock was so great that he died of grief, while his wife put the child down and ran towards him. Overwhelmed, she left his body and came back to the child only to see the boy snatched up by a mysterious and beautiful woman who disappeared with him into the waters of a lake. Cumbrians once claimed this as being Tarn Wadling on the road between Penrith and Carlisle, but it has been drained now. A sad commentary on how the modern world has treated the magic Lady. The Breton tale however explains that this lake was merely an illusion cast for Vivienne by Merlin, but it was enough to fool the mother and so the boy – Lancelot – was brought up by the Lady of the Lake as though he were her own.

Using the terms of the Qabalah then the emotions of Netzach, although capable of perceiving Beauty (Tiphereth), will be expressed only through lust and promiscuity without the self-discipline to balance. So Netzach is balanced as much by Geburah as by Hod. From another viewpoint the science and logic of Hod, although passionately applied by Netzach, will become abominable without the compassion, concern and humour of Chesed.

But that's enough of that.

We can learn more by looking at the 'vice' of this sphere, which is unchastity, or lust. The ancient and little known goddess Flidias manifests this aspect well, for she is chiefly remembered for her insatiable sexual appetite. We are told that only she could satisfy the libido of her husband, Fergus Ro-ech (Fergus, 'son of the Great Horse') whereas it took seven other women to do so. These sexual arts are indicative of her huge store of vitality, and Dion Fortune might almost be writing about Flidias when she discusses the role of the priestesses of Aphrodite. These were trained from childhood in love's skills, we are told, but...

> ...this art was not simply that of provoking passion, but of adequately satisfying it on all levels of consciousness; not simply by the gratification of the physical sensations of the body, but by the subtle etheric exchange of magnetism and intellectual and spiritual polarisation. This lifted the cult of Aphrodite out of the sphere of simple sensuality and explains why the priestesses of the cult commanded respect and were by no means looked upon as common prostitutes, although they received all comers.[10]

Clearly Flidias was able to satisfy Fergus on all levels of activity. She was an artist of love, in full control of the creative energies within her.

In some ways rampant promiscuity is the most unsatisfying thing of all. Basic sexual desires are sated but unless the more mystic aspects of Vivienne are brought into action then we are left in the invidious position of Fergus Ro-ech before he met his wife. It is appropriate therefore that Flidias is also goddess of wild things, and a woodland goddess. She is a counterpart of Cernunnos (the Celtic Pan), the Hidden God of the great forest

which covered most of the country. It is Cernunnos who emerges from the depths of the trees every now and again to stand on the edge of the tilled ground and play us music of the most unutterable longing. Only those who fear passion should fear the gods and goddesses of this sphere.

9.

Moons, Grails and Cauldrons

Few things can be more evocative than a red moon rising. And whether it shines above forest or slum makes no difference, for whichever place receives its lambent light becomes at once beautiful, hypnotic, and tinged with a certain Otherness. We are closer to the Gate at these moments than at any other time.

In astrological terms:

> The Moon factor is the mediator between past and present, accumulating the whole story of man's personal evolution within the fluids of the brain and body; each new experience registered, unconsciously digested and transmuted into instinctive functions...The Moon establishes an essential rhythm in the body and instinctive mind...An ebb and flow that maintains the periodical need for man to withdraw into past experience, memory, or to draw on the past, for the revitalizing of mind and body, as these are revitalized with sleep.[1]

While on the glyph of the Heavenly Man this sphere equates with the reproductive organs, indicating that the concern here is with pure, blind, instinctual sex of almost reptilian levels, free of any thought or glamour. It is the source of power, the raw material of the universe. In the Qabalah the sphere of Yesod (which means 'Foundation') absorbs the downward flowing emanations of the higher spheres and it is here that opposites are resolved.

The Moon-world is that beyond the Gate which we are busy fashioning. Once through there and we fall prey to the feeling of alienation. The young magician feels utterly alone, misunderstood, and scarcely able to relate to the world around. It is an inner landscape which is travelled by means of any self-imposed discipline which might involve some measure of independent activity or self-perpetuated passion.

In everyday terms, the stimulus which will invariably push us deeply into this lunar country is a broken love-affair coupled with a battered and shaken ego. When the brittle shell of the ego begins to crack then it is common for some very odd and hitherto uncharacteristic reactions to emerge. The normally genial wretch finds himself capable of nastiness, is racked by unstoppable internal monologues, and is washed over by endless self-pity. When we go this far along the path we undergo a mild and socially-accepted form of lunacy. We have all been through it. At one time it was said that magical initiations had a comparable effect upon the candidate.

The stages through madness — in the more usual sense — have been described by Joseph Campbell as Separation, Initiation, and Return. Or Moon, Sun and Star according to our present system. This stage of Separation is precisely the moment of encounter with the first inner moon-rise. The binding stresses within the personality snap, the mask falls to pieces; something strange emerges.

In some of the Eastern occult systems exercises are used which specifically aim at 'breaking' the ego. One guru made his over-proud disciple run around the market place on all fours barking like a dog; while Blavatsky did similar to the Bishop Leadbeater when she made him walk the length of a crowded passenger liner carrying a full chamber pot. More fool him.

In contrast to the calculated techniques of such systems the stock experiences of our desperate Western society act as initiating factors in their own right. The strains and neuroses which are peculiar to the West are in themselves means by which we may evolve. After all, the Moon we see is but one-sided: there is also the dark side. The excitement the world felt upon first seeing photographs of the dark side might well be compared with the present fervour man feels in exploring the endlessly dark and pock-marked surfaces that lie behind the mesmeric light of his lunar nature.

In various arcane Hermetic systems this inimical side to man's inner nature was described as the 'Dweller on the Threshold'. It was regarded as a monstrous and malignant entity guarding the gates to the mystical otherworld, and one which had to be defeated before progress could be made. This was, of course, not so much an actual demonic entity but rather a personification of the seeker's own hidden and suppressed shadow self. Upon realizing that the foul beast was none other than himself, his sense of horror became magnified to the point of insanity.

> With the best intentions they 'summoned the Dweller' which often appeared to the Inner eye as a most unpleasant sort of fiend, and attacked it with every weapon suggested by self-righteous virtue. To their amazement and horror, they found themselves sustaining every injury they inflicted on the monster, which made them realize they were wounding themselves, and the monster's face was really a distortion of their own. Many a mind broke under the impact of this appalling revelation. To see the worst of oneself focused into a personalization is a most demoralizing affair.[2]

In other words when we learn to see into our own unconscious for the first time, our very first and most terrifying opponent is the aggregate of our unregenerate and atavistic nature.

Here be dragons, in fact.

Like the Dweller on the Threshold the dragon is a composite of various elements: the serpent with its venom and supposed slime; the bat or eagle wings; the lion claws and breath of fire. It is terrible and irresistible. It is something that we all possess, coiled at the base of the spine, a plumed or winged serpent whose arousal can take us into other worlds. The techniques for achieving this are invariably sexual even when no overt sexual activity is performed.

In his *Alchemical Studies* Jung noted that 'The dragon, or serpent, represents the initial state of unconsciousness, for this animal loves, as the alchemists say, to dwell "in caverns and dark places".' This sexual symbolism is repeated with tales of dragons living under the sea, guarding secret treasure, or more obviously in the many accounts of dragons guarding women tied to stakes.

The primary image of the latter within the English consciousness is that of St George, whom some researchers regard as a manifestation of Arthur. Although the latter never came into such a classic confrontation with a dragon, he did nevertheless achieve renown for pulling the monstrous *addanc* from a lake. The precise nature of this creature is not clear but we do see within the episode a recurrence of the symbolism dealt with here.

Interestingly, in most of the old myths the dragons were usually

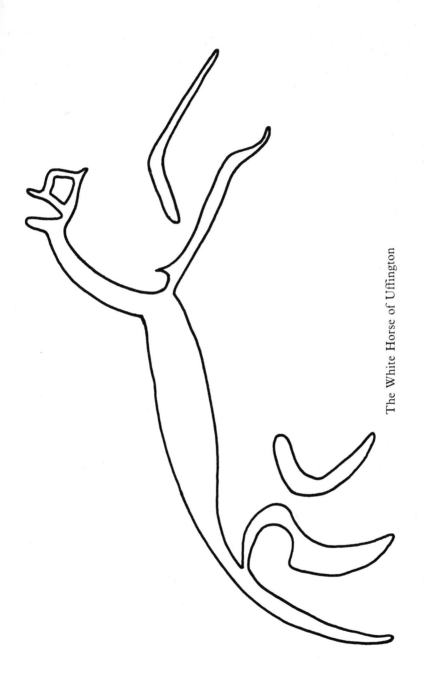

The White Horse of Uffington

slain by the hero or else hard done by. But in the myths of
modern fantasy writers the dragons actively co-operate with the
heroes, as in the loyal fighting dragons of Anne McCaffrey's
Dragon Quest, or with the world-saving brute in Ursula le Guin's
magical book *The Farthest Shore*. Perhaps it is an indication that
the Contraceptive Age looks upon the libido in a far different
light to those societies which insisted upon killing the dragon or
suppressing its force within the psyche. After all, man has now
landed on the Moon. He understands it. It can never arouse the
same awe, fear and mystery of earlier days. So, of course, the
dragon-image is affected. The Greek alchemist Zosimos writing
in the fourth century had his own ideas about handling such a
creature, and it could well be an encounter with the Dweller
which he describes when he exhorts the reader to build a temple
of white lead of infinite dimensions:

> Let it have in its interior a spring of pure water, sparkling like the
> sun...A dragon lies at the entrance guarding the temple. Lay hold
> upon him; immolate him first; strip him of his skin, and taking his
> flesh with the bones, separate the limbs; then, laying the limbs
> together with the bones at the entrance of the temple make a step of
> them, mount thereon, and enter, and you will find what you seek.[3]

Which makes for a very fine description of the magician's
encounter with his Dweller on the astral plane — when it is born
in mind that the astral plane and the unconscious are
synonymous.

The relationship between the dragon and the moon is indicated
in the origins of the former word. It comes from the Greek *drakon*
which means 'to see' or 'to look at'. Like the Man in the Moon
the dragon is constantly watching; it has a power which must be
mastered before we can slip through to gain the golden apples in
the Garden of Hesperides. Which ties in also with the other main
image of Water.

If the dragon symbolizes a composite of our dark selves in
confrontation with normal awareness, then the water symbolism
becomes exquisitely apt. Pools of still water were the first means
by which man could see himself. Life emerged from the sea as life
emerges from the semen. The moon affects the tides as it affects
the menstrual cycle as it is said to affect the mental state of some

people permanently drowning in the shadow lands. Among general beliefs were the moon's role as an abode of dead souls, and the dragon's association with death. A dead man was thought to transform into a dragon, while dragons were regarded as the guardians of treasures in burial chambers.

Wherever we approach the symbols of moon, water, dragon we see the constant associations with death, treasure, darkness, sex and fear. And yet even the most inimical of these can be used to give us another Gate to greater awareness. The dragon-power can tear us apart, yes, but a successful confrontation gives access to immense treasure.

We have already mentioned the possibility of Arthur being a Dragon King in the same sense that some pharaohs were described as being 'winged' — priest-kings who had awakened and utilized the magical potential within. (The symbol of the latters' status could be seen in the uraeus worn upon the brow.) Paul Newman in his excellent book *The Hill of the Dragon* gives a differing opinion, but one which still links this king with the mystical beast:

> King Arthur, whose title 'Pendragon' has been taken as an allusion to the polestar Thuban, which in megalithic times stood at the head of the constellation, Draco. Hence Pendragon or 'head of the dragon' is a legacy of the ancient star-cults.[4]

It is at this point however that we must take stock and realize that we are getting involved with a plurality of Arthurs. The being whose totem was a bear, and the being whose image was a dragon are scarcely likely to be the same person. Rather should we think of them as inheritors of a magical lineage of unchanged essence but different styles. If the secret of the earliest Arthurs was in the dragon-power, then by the time we get to the king of popular romance it has changed into something else: it has changed into the...

Holy Grail

Arthur had created the Round Table and secured the kingdom; he had married and won the respect of all factions; he had done all that a young king could, and yet it was not until the Grail appeared within the Court that they had anything greater than themselves to yearn for. Which is what we all need. The appearance of the Holy Grail and the Quest for the same represent the highest attainment within the Cycle.

Yet no-one is sure what the Grail actually is. All we know is that at Pentecost, when all the seats of the Table were filled, a terrible storm broke the air at night-time. Though it was dark outside a pure sunbeam fell into the hall upon the bowed heads of the knights. Then, floating above them in the light came the glorious vision of the Holy Grail. It was screened from their sight by a cloth of white samite but from it darted rays of light that 'waxed and receded as lightning seems to do'. It passed slowly over their heads and was gone.

The Western psyche has never been the same since.

The most common belief is that the grail was — is — the cup used by Christ at the Last Supper. The natural question then follows: What does it contain? and the answer received is invariably: Everything.

The precedent for this is found in the many Celtic myths based upon Cauldrons. Such as: the cauldron of Keridwen, already described; that of Dagda, from which no-one went unsatisfied; the cauldron of Peredur seen at the court of the King of Sorrows

which could bring the dead back to life with all their faculties; the cauldron of Bran which did exactly the same, except that the faculty of speech was missing; and the cauldron of Mider/Manannan.

In each case the vessel is an image of endless life, either through its bounty or its ability to re-awaken the dead. Likewise in the Grail Banquet the most preferred food miraculously appeared on the plates, while the holy cup itself was held to provide Life Eternal for those who achieved it.

Whatever the cup was, or whatever it contained, it remains the most potent of all the links with the Otherworld. As the Moon is the orb nearest the earth, so is the Grail the stepping-off point most firmly fixed in the cusp between Thisworld and the Otherworld.

Interestingly, in Malory's version its appearance was heralded by a terrible storm. Turbulence of this nature is due to more than mere climatology but are rather indicators of significant transitions between the worlds. It was said to have occurred when Jung died, lightning striking a favourite carved stone in his garden. It happened when the cockney medium known simply as the Boy died in India, as recorded by Swami Omananda. It happened at Calvary too. It is as if the transition of power from one world to the other causes violent rents in the veil of the atmosphere. We can expect storms in the air and in our psyches when the Hawk Gods come, too.

It was Chretien de Troyes who helped create the matrix for all of this, and it is in his words that we can read the earliest and most lovely description of the Grail Procession.

The knights stood in a brilliantly lit hall, filled with blazing torches. While they talked a servant appeared carrying a shining white spear from the point of which a drop of blood whelled, to run down to the servant's hand. After him came two other handsome young men each carrying gold candlesticks of ten candles each. Then after them came the grail, carried by a beautiful, finely dressed maiden. When she appeared it was as though the rising sun had dimmed the star light of the torches. After her came another maiden carrying a silver platter, but the grail which went before was the most beautiful to be found in land or sea, of purest gold set with precious stones.[5]

In the preceding chapters analysing each binary we have already discussed the motifs of the dripping spear, horn, scabbard, sacred matings and the like. It is in the Grail that we find these images being resolved, although initially it seems to project a bewildering variety of possibilities. Geoffrey Ashe writes:

> The Grail stands for a Christian mystery entrusted only to Britain. It is a token of the friendship of God, the vehicle of a special sacrament. Strange rituals are built round it. Secret words are spoken. Visions of Christ and the Virgin are vouchsafed to those who approach the Grail in the right spirit. Not everyone sees them. The Grail sometimes has the air of a *speculum* like the crystal gazer's ball, a channel for the scrying gift which some people possess (whatever the source of the images they see) and others do not.[6]

But the Grail is more than a channel for the scrying gift: it is a channel for souls. It is, in essence, the foundation of that sexual magic which seeks to enter other worlds, or else bring souls into this one. It is here, at the ninth sphere of the Moon, that we get involved in the gestation processes. If we could look into the Grail we would see our ancestors peering back, seeking the right parents for incarnation. This is the Collective Unconscious of Yesod, the basis of all things.

A simple magical exercise might run as follows:

See yourself looking down a long valley, the line of hills at either side of you being bare and pale as flesh, smooth and straight. They join at the valley's end where a cluster of hazel trees spread up the rounded sides a little way. The sky is a silvery violet, there is a gibbous moon rising above the valley's end and you walk toward it. A low mist clings to the ground. You hear the crying of pea-fowl. Two swans fly across the face of the moon. You come to the edge of the thicket and gently touch the standing stone there which seems to hum with life. Moonlight falls between the branches like the pillars of a temple and you discern a narrow path leading off into the trees. You enter the thicket and feel yourself in a world that is crammed with life, that the trees and even the ground beneath are part of the body of some living creature. It is a violet-shadowed, dense and holy place, ancient beyond all telling. The trees give way to a clearing. There is a round deep pond there. You can see the moon upon the face of the waters. You kneel down to look at your own reflection but see instead a myriad of faces — your own departed relatives, your most remote ancestors, and all those people whom you may have hero-worshipped from afar. They are there below the surface of the pool. They are alive, and real. You are now at a point where you can communicate...

The pool itself is a Grail of course, using one interpretation of the latter. It is the Pool of Knowledge where Finn caught the magic Salmon which fed on the nuts dropped from nine hazel trees. It is also an analogue of the womb.

The Grail has now become an important symbol within our Collective Unconscious. By contacting in some slight way this Grail-image we touch upon old yet vital stars within the psyche. Arthur's knights searched for the depths of their Christian heritage when they took their Quests through this moon-country, and it is this subliminal contact with instinctual power and aggregates of consciousness that enables us to progress along our own lines, our lives forging symbols in the astral light which will aid those who follow.

That the Grail as a cup is an obviously feminine symbol we have already noted. M. Esther Harding in her book *Women's*

Mysteries describes the tradition of women leaving their tribes during menstruation for the solitude of the forest. She suggests that modern women might profit by such a symbolic retreat of their own. That is, when the moon-time comes around they should use the physiological and psychological changes as means of retreating and exploring inside themselves.

Which is what is indicated by the Grail Quest. When two knights attain the holy object they make contact with the figure representing the core of their inner heritage. In other words, by descending through our instincts we can reach the bottom of the cup/Grail/ocean/unconscious and reach the very foundation of life. The further down we go the more we become like Merlin or his Enchantress, the more we become Deep Fishers. The method of Merlin is to land his catch through artifice and technique; that of Vivienne is by charming the catch through attraction and empathy.

So this sphere of Yesod is what Lao Tzu would describe as 'The gate of the subtle and profound female' which is the 'root of Heaven and Earth'. It is also the sphere of the unconscious which gives rise to all that we are. The universal symbol describing the latter is of course deep water. From the ocean life first sprang, and water comprises the largest part of bodily weight. The power of the ocean is incalculable; for all practical purposes the depths are unseeable. Unless we are strong, honest and lucky then the creatures which arise now and again can overwhelm us. It happens to magicians when they don the robes of priest-king and go fishing. Most of them end up being swallowed.

Alan Watts was a case in point. He was a man who did more than most to popularize Eastern thought, especially Zen. The title of one of his books sums up his attitude to the mystical quest: *This Joyous Cosmology*. His was a slick, beatific, free-wheeling vision of life which was able to make his readers feel vaguely guilty about their own darker views. An Englishman, he ended up in California (the western-most place on the globe) as a broken, frustrated, and cynical drunk. The waters, and what they contained, claimed him. He would never have got too far as a Grail Knight. But then again only two ever did — Perceval and Galahad.

There is also another interpretation of the Grail which has been convincingly researched and stimulatingly expressed by Messrs,

Baigent, Leigh, and Henry Lincoln in their book *The Holy Blood and the Holy Grail*. In essence their book suggests that Jesus did not die upon the cross, that Mary Magdalen was his wife, that he had children — and that the bloodline survives today cultivated by the mysterious Prieuré de Sion. In the authors' speculation the Holy Grail is linked with the actual blood-descendants of Christ. Quite what this will lead to the authors themselves are not sure, but certainly the Prieuré has been responsible for the manipulation of events on the world's stage. We are reminded here of the occult tradition that high Initiates have the Atlantean bloodline, and that their powers are due to genetic structures rather than psycho-spiritual techniques. How this fits in with our present speculations (if at all) is a matter for individual fancy.

Whichever of the many interpretations one favours we still find this essential link with Life, whether it springs from the cauldron, womb, or the genetic stock of a regal blood-line. Because of this it is also the level of ancestral memory, the recall of which has been practised with varying degrees of reliability by Joan Grant, Christine Hartley, and Arthur Guirdham among the better known seers. The problem here is caused by the sheer malleability of the astral light/unconscious mind. Like water it can assume the shape of whatever vessel holds it. Which makes the recall of past lives one of the most dubious of the occult arts. In my own inspired moments I have been at various times Harold Godwinsson, D.H. Lawrence, John Middleton Murry, Chaka Zulu (*that* one didn't last long), St Ywi, Jesus, Imhotep, and Colonel Seymour himself. Not to mention a variety of troopers in the 82nd Airborne. But I finally accepted that I was not any of them; they were just heroes. Just reflections in my unconscious. It is a stage we all go through and a necessary one in that it links us with our ancient life and heritage. And while I believe that the recall of genuine past lives is possible, I also feel it is not important. In the last analysis we must achieve an independence from such dreams.

In fact within the Qabalah the spiritual 'Virtue' of Yesod is this quality of Independence. It is the strength which comes from a person well on the way toward individuation. The person who has found himself can stand apart; while the reaction of the masses to one such is to actually force him to do so. Interestingly, examples abound of how people who took to living in actual isolation in the wilds developed an increased 'sensitivity' to the things around them. Often this sensitivity developed into real psychism. Perhaps this faculty is becoming prevalent now because of the inner isolation forced upon people by modern society.

In contrast the Qabalistic vice of Yesod is Idleness. This comes from the fear of setting out on the path alone, and/or lack of desire.

People thus afflicted look for the cornucopia aspect of the cauldron, or Grail, hoping to receive all they need without effort. These people are the dabblers in fringe occultism, who consult fortune-tellers for the smallest decision rather than make a choice themselves. These are the people who get stuck on hero-worship or memories of past lives.

May the gods grant that we can win some measure of the dragon-force within to carry ourselves toward our Grails. For this is precisely what we need to rise above the lower world: we must give wings to the primitive power coiled at the bases of our spines; we must become ancient, strong, holy and unique; we must breathe fire to scorch deception, brighten our own paths, and warm the pool of arcane Knowledge bubbling within our spirit; we must slough our dead skin, rise from our deep lairs and head upward.

Moon, Sun and Star...the inescapable route.

10.

The Holy City

Camelot was a dream. The perfect place. It is found in every stone circle, every barrow, every church or glade where man has called passionately upon his gods. It was the perfect place, and still is. The description of Arthur as the Once and Future King can be adapted to every aspect of the Cycle. The castle of Camelot and all that it contained is a blueprint — flawed perhaps, but all the more enduring and endearing because of it. Crowley used a similar blueprint to create his Abbey of Thelema at Cefalu; Gurdjieff with his Prieuré at Fontainebleau; Dion Fortune with her Society of the Inner Light off the Bayswater Road. Where men and women of any persuasion have sought to manifest their highest ideals in physical terms, then that material basis is given the aura of Camelot by the aspirations behind the brickwork. Camelot has become the temple of Western dreams where attempts were made to bring down God into the world.

In the system of Qabalah we are concerned with the sphere of Malkuth, which means 'Kingdom'. It is the earth on which we live, and the physical body. The latter, in fact, has long been regarded as the 'temple of the living God', and the old Initiates used to cry: 'There is no part of me that is not also a part of the Gods!' The seed and the flower cannot be separated, nor can God and man, nor can Arthur and Camelot.

That city was, and is, a channel through which certain spiritual aspects of the psyche could function. In various magical techniques the operator begins by building up in his imagination the outline of a temple. He fashions it according to his will and thence proceeds toward his inner light. The temple becomes a symbolic starting point. It is a means of finding one's way from normal consciousness to more sublime states and safely back again. When a magician fashions a simple temple in actuality it is not the physical objects which are of particular importance, but the unconscious associations. In other terms Malkuth (Camelot) is just dull matter without Yesod (dreams).

> For while Malkuth is essentially the sphere of form, all coherence of parts, save simple mechanical stresses and electro-magnetic attractions and repulsions, depend upon the functions of Yesod. And Yesod, though it is essentially a form-giving Sephirah, depends for the manifestation of its activities upon the substance provided by Malkuth. The forms of Yesod are 'such stuff as dreams are made of' till they have picked up the material particles of Malkuth to body forth their forms.[1]

This is where we find the 'dragon under the hill', for if the former creature represents the hot vital force of life, the image of the hill depicts the actual physical matter thus vitalized. Many of the ancient Egyptian temples were architectural representations of the human body. The old stone circles of Europe and their attendant complexes such as at Avebury and Silbury Hill were representations of the symbiosis between Nature and Woman. The Yorkshire painter Monica English describes her visions of the rituals attending such cult centres which involved processional movements, chants, and many fires.

> The idea was deliberately to make the circle powerful by pouring out their own emotions, and they did it so efficiently that you can still feel it there now. But at the time it was all to do with the preparation for the entrance of the Goddess Queen. The reverence in which she was held was enormous. The circle protected her, but somehow at the same time allowed the life force to enter her and be concentrated in her. All the ritual was to lead up to the great moment when she was possessed and made her pronouncements like an oracle. It was to do with the fertility of nature, the safety of the cattle, the welfare of the people, that sort of thing – the original witchcraft, the natural sort, not at all the invented witchcraft which is around today.[2]

Avebury of course was a very powerful prototype for Camelot. Arthur Guirdham's revenants told him that the former still acts as a centre which draws into itself the inimical forces of the surrounding area and transmutes them into something more benign. F.P.D. had a powerful vision of his own which was written up as follows:

Feb. 13th 1939. C.C.T. and self. *Time* 8.30 – 9 p.m. Room was very quiet and had been carefully sealed beforehand. Both very fit. Dark of moon near, weather fine and spring like.

1. Waited for about 5 minutes and picked up a place that looked Avebury as it may have been say 3000 or 4000 years ago, except there was a long altar stone in the middle and over it had been built a sort of roof of leaves that looked like beech. It was very early in the morning just after the dawn and I think it was about Beltaine. I noticed the dew on the grass. Then came two priests one carrying a gold hilted bronze (?) sword about $2\frac{1}{2}$ feet long. This was a big man heavily built with a wide face a big mouth, large teeth with very prominent and pointed eye teeth. The other was a smaller man, thin and fanatical looking who carried a large gold cup. Following them were men carrying a rough litter on which lay a young woman about 20 or 30. Fair hair blue eyes. She was naked with fingernails, toe nails, and nipples painted red. She was not bound.

(*Note* I was feeling awful my back all creepy and I was unable to move in my chair.) Then the woman was placed on the altar stone with her head (face) facing N.E. looking into a notch in the hills where the sun would appear. This woman was paralysed below the neck or hypnotised or drugged. But she could move her head a little and her eyes rolled, and she was fully conscious. The big priest stood behind her head waiting for the sun to rise to plung the sword between the painted nipples. The smaller priest with the bowl squatted at her feet to catch the blood from a runnel in the gently sloping stone of sacrifice. The whole temple space was filled with figures. The sun came up after a long wait, the priest raised the sword to stab and I recognised him as DNF, the other was Chris and I was the girl sacrificed on the stone. The big priest had the face of a devil. I ended dead beat both physically and emotionally.

A psychologist could make much of that, but I believe that he would be wrong; or worse still, unproductive. Our concern here is to show that while those two magicians were ostensibly doing no more than sitting in chairs before a gas fire, in their most exalted and inward reality they were witnessing rites performed in a temple that exists beyond Time. Whether it was an accurate memory of Willing Sacrifice at Avebury or some Freudian upsurge is not, ultimately, important. Brodie-Innes who ran the Golden Dawn temple in Edinburgh once said that whether the gods existed or not is irrelevant, for the point was that the universe behaved as though they did. We might adapt this to the foregoing and add that whether Camelot functioned as legend has it, is unimportant, for the psyche would have it that it did.

Ritualists are generally not content with visions of temples that existed in pre-history, but invariably create something in their spare rooms which can represent their magical natures. How an outsider might respond to such is entirely subjective, even though holiness as a force can be as tangible as electricity. (And given some of the theories of dowsers it may even *be* electric in essence.) Christine Hartley loves the Tor at Glastonbury but it leaves me flat and bored. Guirdham's psychic associates were often made physically ill near churches which reek of sanctity to others. There is a valley in Northumberland which is Most Holy to me but means nothing to anyone else. We respond to the earth and its temples in different ways.

So the actual brick and mortar of Camelot is considerably less important than the associations. It is the act of building such a place that gives rise to the work which Gurdjieff described as the only real magic. Hatha Yoga as a means of spiritual development is useless unless each posture is linked with some higher principle.

Not all of us, however, have the wherewithal to create a temple. Not all of us have spare rooms. In these cases the effective temple can be created in the imagination. Crowley, who wished to invoke the gods in the middle of China knew that while it was impossible to get to his temple at Boleskine, Scotland, he could certainly bring the same to him. In doing similar ourselves it often helps to use at least some physical stimulus to attune the mind. It can be as simple as a clean sheet spread on the floor; or facing East, from where the magical current is said to flow; or uttering some self-created Word. The actual shape of the temple is then built up in the imagination according to taste. When the Inner Light was functioning at its height the forms were essentially Egyptian. The system of magic created by W.E. Butler uses an Arthurian castle, a miniature Camelot. Personal fancy is likely to suggest each person's own temple. Years ago, when the original draft of this was written, my mind took to its own meandering: I was pleasantly obsessed with the fantasy of a tower, like Thoor Ballylee, and how I would renovate it, where I would put windows and stairs. It was a compulsion which had no links with probability owing to a certain affliction known as penury. It did, however, develop into my own astral temple which is essentially a Border pele tower, surrounded by a moat, the inside of which is simple indeed. Inside that place is warmth, light, and comfort. Nothing much magical occurs there because I am not a magician. There are no stellar trips, no divine invocations. But in a chaotic world it is the one secure place, stuck in the centre of my psyche, where things are as they *should* be, where nothing inimical can enter and only healing occur. In times of hurt or darkness I go to this place and curl up before the fire which burns on the southern side, close my eyes and go to sleep. Perhaps in time there will be room in there for calling down the gods, too, but not just yet. For the time being it is my walled sanctuary, my own Camelot. It will be a long time, if ever, before I go out riding.

If there is a multitude of Arthurs then the same holds true of Camelot. It exists in Cornwall, Somerset, Wales, Scotland, Cumbria and Brittany. It has always been a moveable city. In the last century, when the population became unprecedentedly mobile because of the developments in transport, the main centre for mystic cities generally was Africa. Tintagel and the like were momentarily forgotten. A holy place is not without honour save in its own country. Africa, then, gradually became the focus for the imaginations of the popular fiction writers such as Edgar Rice Burroughs, and especially H. Rider Haggard. The latter evoked gleaming white cities ruled from central palaces within which we might find 'She Whose Name May Not Be Spoken', an eternal, ageless woman. Right in the heart of the Dark Continent. Had mankind itself stayed still the public imagination would see them there yet, but unfortunately Africa the unknown continent became, for all practical purposes, Known. So those simple paradises utilizing alternative technology where the natives fell down before the bewildered explorer as though he were a god, had to be moved. Tibet was in vogue for a long time. It still is among some, although the Communist invasion and satellite photography have dented many hopes of there really being magical cities amid the snowy peaks. People have seen their Camelots within the Andes, such as in the Shangri-la type valley purportedly run by the 'Brotherhood of the Seven Rays'. Many intelligent people have been — and are — convinced that our globe is hollow, and that a super-race exists within it. But as Earth became more and more explored, the most viable alternative was presented by the science fiction writers who postulated a new home at the other side of the sky. When this genre began to boom there was almost a collective sigh of relief from the readers. A City of Hope was still possible after all.

But only for a few decades. By the time the American and Russian space programmes began to wind down the public had already grasped that escape to the stars en masse was not as likely as it had once seemed. And so they turned inward. They used on one level the fantasy writings of Tolkien or Michael Moorcock; on another level they sought the gratuitous grace of LSD. Often they used both. And Crowley's books began to sell again.

All because man needs to believe in Another Place which, depending on his predilection, is either within or without, the albedo of its whitened walls determined by the desperate intensity of his own light.

The Irish in their wisdom had more than one centre. They had their Four Holy Cities from which came the mighty race of the Tuatha de Danann, children of the Goddess Danu. There was:

Gorias   in the east, the place of the rising sun, from whence came the spear of the sun-god Lugh.

Finias   the southern city, from whence Nuada brought his Sword of Light.

Murias   in the west from which was brought Undry, Dagda's famous cauldron described as 'a hollow filled with water and fading light'. It seems that in Wales this place was called Morvo, and in France Morois.

Falias   was the northern city from which came Fal, the Stone of Destiny, said to cry out when the rightful King of Ireland stood upon it.

Actually, Hartley places the sword in the east and the spear in the south thus according with the scheme of modern magic, but the important thing is that both these 'weapons' are in the positive, dynamic half of the circle (east and south) while the cauldron and the stone are in the passive and receptive quarters. More of this presently.

In the system of Qabalah we find that Malkuth has no astrological planet as have the other spheres. Instead it is equated with the 'Sphere of the Elements' which relates directly with these Four Cities. Were we to compress these into one to fit our Arthurian scheme, then we could visualize Camelot as being four-gated: a gate of Life, of Light, of Love, and Learning.

Either way we would still equate with the Elements of Air, Fire, Water and Earth respectively. Which brings us to the concept of the tools or 'weapons' which we use to build our temples or win our Quests.

The Wand of Fire

Fire was regarded by early man as the principal element. Even today, faced with the prospect of nuclear fire from above, it has a certain plangent appeal. To the cave-dwellers it offered protection, both as a weapon against beasts and as a barrier against the cold. Discipline and organisation was needed to keep the communal fire lit at all times. In subtle ways it altered the social behaviour and structure of the tribe for it extended his leisure time. After the food gathering had been accomplished and darkness fell he could still see and it was now warm. He could think about developing his tools and weapons. He could dabble in art. The communal fire became a focus for the tribe, and evenings were spent pooling the knowledge and experience each had gained in the day. Sexual habits were probably altered. Fire brands were used for night forays, and more complex methods of tool-making developed using the properties of fire. The simple fire-hardened stick became a potent weapon and could also be used as a means of controlling the camp-fires and raking up the embers. Hence the Wand.

The prevalance of fire in religious worship is self-evident. Candles are burned on altars; smoke from incense rises to the heavens and carries our prayers with it.

Fire can purify and it can consume. It can illuminate or destroy.

The Cup of Water

The complement to Fire. Man can survive for long periods without food as long as he drinks water. Until the recent advent of piped water all communities had to be near some source of that substance. In countries where it was scarce it became venerated. Water, as the ocean, is regarded as the source of life on earth. We crawled out of the sea billions of years ago and evolved into the creatures we are now. It was once the only substance which could subdue fire, and could also be used in conjunction with fire to help crack large rocks into manageable fragments. It offered also the first means of expanding man's horizons by anything other than his feet – that is by boat. There was also the connection with life and death: lives would drain away with the red liquid; life would be born following the bursting of a woman's water; animals would gather at the local water-hole. Water could also offer man the first glimpse of what he was. Unlike fire it does not have to scorch a thing pure but can do so benignly. A man could submerge himself without harm – something he could never do with fire. It depicts the fluid emotions and feelings within us, which pour into the shapes provided by those we need, depend on and love. Hence the Cup, or magical Scabbard.

The Sword of Air
Here we find intellect, the capacity for thought. In a literal sense air is necessary as a medium for speech and hearing, which are both faculties for implementing the intellect. At the very beginning speech came before thought. Air actually inspired its own directing source. That is, the prehistoric grunt meaning 'no' came before the abstract concept within the grunter's mind. From speech came the shared experience with others. In its most divine expression we find it in the Word, the single utterance which began everything. The magical Sword was perhaps originally the arrow, Gray feels. Which is an obvious Air attribution. The sword however became the aristocrats weapon, a prestige device which required the highest technology available. A technology built upon intellect, enquiry, and an outward-seeking attitude. In the Arthurian Cycle it is Merlin who is responsible for giving the swords to Arthur. He is the protoscientist passing on the power of what he has discovered. The Sword is also a scalpel, it is pen-nib. It is a fast means of expressing things. It requires skill to use it with optimum effect.

The Shield of Earth
This device was once, according to Gray, a prototypal spade. Which links us with the solid substance of everyday life. The Elements can be redefined as Gases, Radiations, Liquids, and Solids. It is the latter which concerns us now. By Earth we mean our bones, flesh, the bricks of our houses, the wood of the trees and the soil beneath us.

When man first learned to till the ground and understand

something about crops, his previously nomadic hunting-gathering existence came to an end. His life began to assume some measure of stability. He would use his spade to work the soil, he would live near water, he could control fire and even create the same. His tools were relatively sophisticated. This element thus represents solidity, security. Cut a segment from a globe and you have a shield. Galahad won a magical version of one with a bleeding cross in the middle. It reminds us of the Gnostic or Buddhist ideas that man's soul entrapped in Matter must necessarily know Sorrow. The knightly ritual of demanding combat by striking the hanging shield of an opponent is an image of the war within the psyche when the dynamic aspects clash against the passive.

Each knight was thus equipped when he left Camelot on his Quest. Before we ourselves leave our astral temples we must be similarly armed with an understanding of our Elemental natures. The more magical the knight the more especial his weapons. We have mentioned Galahad's shield, and there is also Arthur's mystic spear known in the Welsh tradition as Ron. Excalibur, or Caliburn is universally known but the real power was in the scabbard which could heal all wounds.

I myself being a Scorpio with Cancer ascendant have a natural affinity with Water, and the cup/scabbard. The sea fascinates me and terrifies. I am afraid of deep water.

We all must become aware of which Weapon most nearly expresses our inner nature. Then the rest can fall into place accordingly.

Traditional magicians give complex details as to how these artefacts might be constructed. Not only how, but when. The Wand, for example, must be made of a particular wood, cut in a certain way at an especial time when the planets are propitious. The effectiveness of each Weapon becomes proportional to the work that goes into making it. Which is true for magic generally. So each Weapon is a physical representation of certain aspects of the psyche. Each one is used to connect the magician's unconscious with the Collective Unconscious. They become means of making contact with the power-sources within/beyond the physical. They help us reach the stars under the earth.

The associations can be given as follows:

Fire	Wand	South	Arthur	Summer
Air	Sword	East	Merlin	Spring
Water	Scabbard	West	Nimue	Autumn
Earth	Shield	North	Morgan	Winter

And so on into infinity. The more attributions that one can link with each Element and Weapon, the more energy that one can evoke.

To recapitulate then: Malkuth equates with the physical realm, with Camelot, with the magical Lodge: it is composed of the Elements which are expressed by the four Weapons. It is in fact All and Everything, the end and therefore the Beginning. It is the womb and tomb, the cave under the hill where Arthur and his knights lie, neither living nor dead, awaiting the Call or the first stirrings of a racial need.

In point of fact it is very easy to give directions to Camelot: it can be found at the precise place where the serpent's mouth clamps around its tail. For by Camelot is meant the whole epic up until and including Arthur's slow journey in the death-barge down to Avalon, the three Queens attending him. The moment that he is laid to rest our own magical journey begins. In a sense each one of us is Arthur. We are figures of Majesty but fallen ones, lying supine in a state of living death on a stone slab in a dark cave beneath a hill. We wait for someone to open the mystic Gate for us and give us some reason to open our eyes. And the knights were no better: they would do nothing at their assembly on Pentecost until some miracle had occurred which could be read as a Sign.

Which on second thoughts is not that unreasonable an attitude. Even the great magicians who were born with profound Gifts and easy contact with the Otherworld have moments of doubt. If the gods want to use us lesser endowed souls then perhaps it is not wrong of us to expect something in the way of a Sign. If truth were known, though, we probably get them all the time except that modern man has lost the art of interpreting omens and making the natural phenomena relay messages. So all we can do is go on asking, listen very quietly, and work very hard. These are the secrets of High Magic. Added to this we can go to those ancient stones which tap the dragon-power beneath the earth and make ourselves open to whatever might eventually filter through.

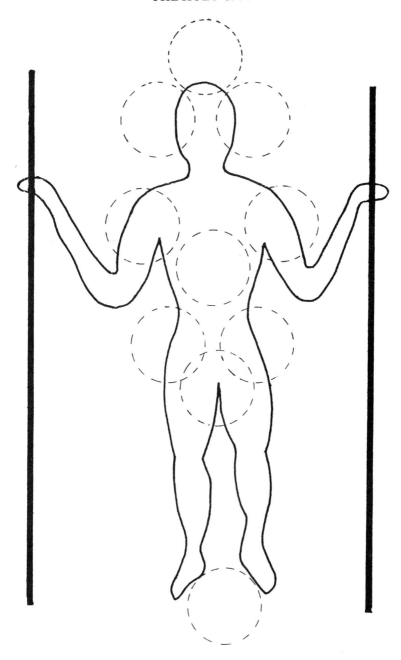

Too often though, we expect the Sign to come in the form of words, as expressed by some charismatic personality expounding a neat philosophy. But it was those men around the table who got it right: they followed white harts, roe deer, hounds, ravens and Questing Beasts – whatever they were. They were in the tradition of the bards and druids and knew that every animal, plant and bird had a deep symbolic meaning and that the right path to the gods could be found if read properly. The ancient Song of Amergin expressed something of this:

> I am a hawk on a cliff
> I am fair among flowers
> I am a god who sets the head afire with smoke
> I am a battle-waging spear
> I am a salmon in the pool
> I am a hill of poetry
> I am a ruthless boar
> I am a threatening noise of the sea
> I am a wave of the sea
> Who but I knows the secrets of the unhewn dolmen?[3]

In the esoteric scheme of the magical Qabalah the 'Spiritual Experience' of this tenth sphere is described as the Knowledge and Conversation of the Holy Guardian Angel. We can alter this a little to read the Knowledge and Conversation of the Holy Mother Earth. With the right application it will be found that She will speak to us in ways that the bards would have understood and that we must learn. Personally, the most profound and poignant moment that I have known was ushered in by the symbol of a black dog. It is a tale irrelevant to anyone else, a meaningless symbol to all but myself. Yet the confluence of Time, Space and Events was such that it was a true sending from the Otherworld. More than any occult tome, that black dog which came to me down a narrow cobbled street in Bath took me nearer to the Gate of Moon than I had ever been before. And now I look for it everywhere.

11.

And Now...?

The great rites of the Cycle came to an end. The magicians of Camelot had drawn down the power and in the main destroyed themselves by doing so. They all died happily every after — which is the prerequisite for charging a myth with energy. Arthur floated off to Avalon, or *avallach*, the garden of apples; Galahad and Perceval entered Castle Carbonek and stepped into the Otherworld forever; the remainder of the knights perished in the dust at Camlann. Apart from Sir Bedivere that is, the Guardian, who was ultimately persuaded to part with Excalibur, the dark fires had destroyed them all.

Except for two: Lancelot and Guinevere. They both took Holy Orders. Which would be laughable had it been the first time that magicians had recanted on their death beds and sought re-admission into the Church. This is the occult formula known as the Hedging of the Bet. So much of the more ostentatious aspects of modern magic is essentially a reaction against society. Although trivial levels of power might be exercised there is little more of the arcane involved than an adolescent desire to shock mummy. Even Crowley was reported as having made the off-hand comment that everything he did was with the intention of shocking his dead mother. The popular expressions of magic are probably more closely related to the middle-class ambience of home-made bread, wine, and Laura Ashley than to any potent contact with the iron of the Old Gods. It is activity in the right direction, but a Qabalist might describe these media-conscious tin adepts as being at the level of Kether in Malkuth, not Malkuth in Kether as they would secretly suppose. Yeats (who as a magician may have been short on power but long on wisdom) once said of a pagan rite he had witnessed that the participants called upon the ancient gods with such fervour and ecstasy that there could be no doubting they were orthodox Christians.

If Guinevere failed in her magical marriage to Arthur, then by entering a convent she thought to try another formula to bring through the power: that of a spiritual marriage to Christ. Likewise Lancelot with Mary. Yet even by Malory's time when the Cycle had been forever Christianized, there are odd clues to the pagan background: Guinevere was said to have retired into the seclusion of a convent near Amesbury. That is to say, almost within sight of Stonehenge. One non-occult writer insisted that this name was the original of Avebury. Either way, Saturn or the Sun, it presents an arcanum to be understood. The White Shadow and the Knight of the Lake had their first death (of the physical body) within the arms of the Church; their Second Death — the withdrawal of the spirit into its essence — took place within the light of the gods they had sought to invoke. By this time all that remained of the Great Hall in Camelot where the best men in the world saw the Holy Grail, was an empty room. Which, of course, is the true and ineffable secret within the Holy of Holies.

In tombs of the elite in ancient Egypt were found spinning tops, which were more than simple toys. As Lucie Lamy comments:

> But spinning discs and cones, as well as the earth itself, have the following 'gyrostatic' property: Any body turning rapidly around its axis tends to orient itself parallel to the earth's axis and its axis swings round in the same direction as the earth' revolution.[1]

Which is a phenomenon that assumes significance when one considers that the Gnostic sect known as the Peratae (a name meaning Those Who Pass Through) discovered...

> ...in the constellation of the Serpent or the Dragon the very meaning of the genesis of the cosmos. It is a curious constellation, one of the most vast in the boreal sky, yet one to which little attention is paid. It stretches its sinuous shapes between Ursa Major and Ursa Minor, its tail lost in the direction of Gemini, its triangular head pointed toward the pole star...Coiled as it is round the northern pole, as if sucking on the navel of the sky, one can understand why it should quickly become charged with symbolic importance.[2]

Stele of the Serpent King from Abydos

Those spinning tops point us back to our recurrent themes of dragon, pole star, cycles, and bears, and we find within the very tip of that spinning device the nature of the first sphere upon the Tree of Life, namely Kether (which means the Crown), symbolized by the Point, or the Point within the Circle. It is also known as the Primum Mobile or the First Stirrings. We could refer to it also as Hu, Lir, Arachne, Danu, or even the ghastly Jehovah. It is whatever we can conceive of as being Ultimate, and at this level it is equally Arthur's 'Vision of Albion'.

It was the latter which motivated the king in all he did. He wanted the crown of Britain to be a means whereby the whole nation could be brought that much closer to God. From the crown emanated all the highest qualities of Power, Compassion, Justice, Mercy, Intuition and Knowledge. After his coronation as the rightful king he drew from his vision the concepts which he attempted to apply to the material reality of his realm. This in fact is a literal example of the way Kether begins to emanate and make its presence felt on the lower worlds. The Crown as it was established within Camelot became an intermediary between the masses and their god. Magically speaking, Tiphereth has been described as the highest sphere that one can attain while conscious; thus Arthur is the highest figure that a commoner could approach with his yearnings. Behind him there was only god.

Kether is, as Fortune wrote, the 'primary concept'. The tarot cards which associate are the Aces, described as: the Root of the Powers of Fire, the Root of the Powers of Water, and so on. AE gives us an esoteric analysis of Dana which is very much in keeping with the nature of Kether.

So is Dana the basis of the material form from the imperishable body of the immortals to the transitory husk of the gnat. As this divinity emerges from its primordial state of ecstatic tenderness or joy in Lir, its divided rays, incarnate in form, enter on a three-fold life of spiritual love, of desire, and the dark shadow of love.[3]

Lancelot would have understood all of that.

AE, or George Russell, went on to analyse the figure of Lir, or Llyr, who is a curious being and apparently a sea-god of some importance, as was his son Manannan, or Manawyddan. Russell comes very close here to representing the dark face of God hinted at by the traditional Magical Image of Kether which is 'an ancient bearded king, seen in profile':

> In the beginning was the boundless Lir, an infinite depth, an invisible divinity, neither dark nor light, in whom were all things past and to be...Of Lir but little may be affirmed, and nothing can be revealed...an infinite being, neither spirit nor substance but rather the spiritual form of these, in which all the divine powers raised above themselves exist in a mystic union or trance. This is the night of the gods from which Manannan first awakened, the most spiritual divinity known to ancient Gael, being the Gaelic equivalent to that Spirit which breathed upon the face of the waters...Manannan is still the Unuttered Word, and is in that state the Chaldaic Oracle of Proclus saith of the Divine Mind; 'it had not yet gone forth, but abode in the Paternal Depth, and in the Dytum of god-nourished silence'.[4]

Which is a perfect description of Kether on the point of manifestation. If light could be poised just like a drop of water poised to drip from a tap, then that is a fair image to work with. Lir is here described as being almost the God behind God, or the Nothingness of the Qabalistic concept of 'Ain Soph Aur'. Lir's children by his first wife were turned into four swans which were doomed to travel the world for a near eternity until such a time as Christianity appeared within Ireland. While the children of Dana became the Tuatha de Danann who had their four holy cities. Perhaps if we were to attribute a single figure within the Arthurian scheme to Kether rather than any Vision, it would be Uther. It has to be him. Unfortunately the little we know about him is scandalous, and in this light he is scarcely a figure capable of symbolizing the Most High. That apart, we do find that the names Uther and Arthur are very similar, which does something to support the notion that the latter is an initiatic title handed down from each Adept to his 'magical son'. If Arthur was a Sacred King then so was Uther before him, and viewed in this respect the senior figure comes across as potent and brooding as Morgan, but with an almost cthonic quality that she lacks. If a magician were to make contact with Uther then he would find himself linking with the Cycle at a point before the Christian gloss had been applied. He will get back to the pagan origins behind Arthur.

Which is about all that can be said of Kether for it is an individual thing. How each man views his High God can be likened to how St Augustine viewed Time: he knew what it was, but when he came to describe it he could not. Kether is beyond our reach on earth except by viewing symbolisations of reflections of shadows. We climb toward those levels blindly.

It is here that the Qabalah is a drawback. For all its marvellous flexibility its pattern still suggests an ordered vertical route. Hence the ludicrous system of Grades within the magical lodges. These were (and still are) essentially as follows:

Kether	– Ipsissimus
Chockmah	– Magus
Binah	– Magister Templi
Chesed	– Adeptus Exemptus
Geburah	– Adeptus Major
Tiphereth	– Adeptus Minor
Netzach	– Philosophus
Hod	– Practicus
Yesod	– Theoricus
Malkuth	– Zelator

Needless to say at Tiphereth there comes a mad scramble to go a step higher: for who would want to be an **Adeptus Minor** when with a little more study Adeptus Major can be attained? Regardie in his book *My Rosicrucian Adventure* described the incompetence of many of the senior Adepts he met within the Golden Dawn, which was why he published almost the entire teachings of that Order but only on the condition that he took no royalties and made no profit from so doing. By throwing this information into the Outer Court, so to speak, it removed the authority of those magicians whose status rested upon their own claims, rather than achievement.

The truth is that the Spheres describe function, not status. Geburah is not superior to Yesod. A Priest of Mars is as potent as a Priest of the Moon but in a differing way. The days of the Grades are over, thankfully. There are only initiates and Initiates, and it is up to each person to decide whether he is a capital or lower case type when he understands that the word only means 'begin'. We are all beginners, then, who know that we work *all* the paths of the Tree *at the same time,* not in any linear sequence.

There are other things that can be done within the QBL apart from scrapping the Grades. The system needs someone able to change the Hebraic God-names into Gaelic or Welsh or Breton equivalents; it needs someone to work out some flexible animal and bird Correspondences, and research more deeply into the lore of serpents, bears, bulls and name origins. What has been presented so far in this book is no more than the froth on waves.

Although I doubt if anyone will do anything much for a long time, if at all, for magicians have always been a pig-headed lot. Yet I am reminded, too, that in ancient times the pig was the most sacred of beasts.

Which brings us to the end of the book as I write these words in my note-pad sitting in the Ichthus café in the hour before I go to work — a location and event deliberately engineered to create Significance. For as I sit here the Age of the Fishes is almost done and I am chilled by the approaching shadow of the Man Carrying Water. I look through the manuscript with a mixture of pleasure and weariness overlaid with uncertainty. It has gone through a dozen incarnations, rejected by innumerable publishers, all of whom felt that there was little public interest in this sort of thing. Perhaps they are right. Even the occult fraternity will not be too enamoured of some of my attitudes. They could argue that I am setting Occultism's reconciliation with Science back at least fifty years. Qabalists meanwhile will see that my Qabalah is weak, magicians that my magic is non-potent, Celtic scholars that my learning is superficial and cribbed, while objective readers will detect a certain ambiguity of sympathy. The whole thing is, I confess, idiosyncratic. It would not be too strong to say that students would be fools to take my attributions for granted. They did that with Crowley's 777 and magic is still recovering. They must work at each image themselves until they get some response. Though I would offer the advice that the idiosyncratic approach is the only one which can ever get much sense from the burning bush of god's spirit which will say no more of itself than: I AM THAT I AM.

It is finished now, contract signed, deadline met, the Old Gods written out of me. They have been clustered around all my life, in one form or another, becoming almost tangible in the past years when their voices were insistent that I place them into the Tree which was slowly burning within my psyche. So I did this, I rammed those dry figures in like kindling and watched the coloured fire in its ten variations, knowing that a part of myself was aflame too. We burned away together during my travels across the Abyss that is America, during a dozen jobs, during the destruction of marriage, during the raptures and torments of a seven year period when the atoms of my body were completely renewed according to one occult theory. The usual sort of thing. It is finished now and I am weary. I will do nothing more dynamic in magic than watch for hawks and talk to ravens. I have listened to the whispers from beyond the keyhole and opened as best I can the Moongate of the cave in which Pendragon sleeps. Let him and his Old Gods come riding out at their leisure and let the witches and magi of this century go galloping off in their own Wild Hunt for whatever nourishment they want these figures to give.

God speed and luck to them all.

References

Introduction
1. Dion Fortune, *Psychic Self Defence* (Aquarian Press 1967), p.19.
2. See: A.J. Stewart, *Died 1513, Born 1929* (Macmillan 1978).
3. See: Arthur Guirdham, *The Cathars and Reincarnation* and *The Island* (Neville Spearman Ltd. 1980).
4. William Irwin Thompson, *The Time Falling Bodies Take to Light* (Rider and Co. 1981), p.3.
5. As Above, p.5.

Chapter 1.
1. Christine Hartley, *A Case for Reincarnation* (Robert Hale 1972), p.76.

Chapter 2.
1. Merlin Stone, *The Paradise Papers* (Virago Ltd. 1976), p.177.
2. C.G. Jung, *Mysterium Coniunctionis* (Bollingen Foundation), p.361.
3. William Irwin Thompson, *The Time Falling Bodies Take to Light*, p.165.
4. Christine Hartley, *The Western Mystery Tradition* (Aquarian Press 1968), p.57.
5. C.G. Jung, *The Archetypes and the Collective Unconscious*, p.102.
6. M. Esther Harding, *Women's Mysteries* (Rider 1971), p.103.
7. Kahlil Gibran, *The Prophet* (Alfred Knopf 1974), p.28.
8. Quoted in Jean Markale's *Women of the Celts* (Gordon Cremonesi 1975), p.137.
9. Dion Fortune, *Moon Magic* (Aquarian Press 1976), p.70.
10. As above, p.40.

11. Robert Graves, *The White Goddess* (Faber 1981), pp.142–143.

Chapter 3.
1. Teilhard de Chardin, *The Future of Man.*
2. Henry Treece, *Hounds of the King* (Bodley Head 1971), p.148.
3. W.G. Gray, *The Inner Traditions of Magic* (Aquarian Press 1970), pp.49–51.
4. William Irwin Thompson, *The Time Falling Bodies Take to Light*, p.224.
5. Deirdre Green and J.A. Johnston from their magazine *Inner Keltia.*
6. Jean Markale, *Women of the Celts* (Gordon Cremonesi 1975), p.242.
7. Robert Graves, *The White Goddess* (Faber 1981), p.389.
8. Eileen O'Faolain, *Irish Sagas and Folk Tales* (OUP 1973), p.64.
9. Mircea Eliade, *Images and Symbols* (Harvill Press 1961), p.45.

Chapter 4.
1. Jeff Mayo, *Teach Yourself Astrology* (EUP Ltd. 1968), p.33.
2. Kenneth Grant, *Aleister Crowley and the Hidden God* (Muller 1973), p.53.
3. As above, p.19.
4. W.G. Gray, *The Ladder of Lights* (Helios 1968), p.81.
5. Aleister Crowley, *Confessions* (Bantam Books 1971), p.421.
6. Dion Fortune, *The Mystical Qabalah* (Ernest Benn 1974), p.183.
7. As above, p.184.

Chapter 5.
1. Jeff Mayo, *Teach Yourself Astrology* (EUP Ltd. 1964), p.34.
2. W.G. Gray, *The Ladder of Lights* (Helios 1968), p.132.
3. Perceval le Gallois p.191, translated Foulet, Stock 1947
4. Josephine Johnson, *Florence Farr* (Colin Smythe 1975), p.75.
5. William Irwin Thompson, *The Time Falling Bodies Take to Light*, p.150.

6. W.G. Gray, *The Ladder of Lights* (Helios 1968), p.135.
7. Elisabeth Haich, *Initiation* (Unwin 1979), p.140.
8. W.G. Gray, *The Ladder of Lights* (Helios 1968), p.135.
9. Warren Kenton, *The Tree of Life* (Rider 1972), p.167.
10. As above, p.115.
11. Arthur Guirdham, *Beyond Jung* (Village Press 1974), p.12.
12. Dion Fortune, *Moon Magic* (Aquarian Press 1976), p.147.
13. See Dillon and Chadwick's, *The Celtic Realms*.
14. W.G. Gray, *The Talking Tree* (Weiser NY 1977), p.253.
15. Kenneth Grant, *Aleister Crowley and the Hidden God* (Muller 1973), p.54.
16. William Irwin Thompson, *The Time Falling Bodies Take to Light*, p.254.

Chapter 6.
1. Colin Wilson, *The Stargazers*.
2. W.G. Gray, *The Rollright Ritual* (Helios 1975), p.66.
3. Dion Fortune, *The Mystical Qabalah* (Ernest Benn), p.211.
4. Dillon and Chadwick, *The Celtic Realms*, p.157.
5. Dion Fortune, *Moon Magic* (Aquarian Press 1976), p.117.

Chapter 7.
1. Jeff Mayo, *Teach Yourself Astrology* (EUP) p.27.
2. Christine Hartley, *The Western Mystery Tradition*, p.50.
3. W.G. Gray, *The Ladder of Lights*, p.60.
4. Lewis Spence, *The Magic Arts in Celtic Britain*, p.35.
5. Marie-Louise Franz, *C.G. Jung, His Myth in Our Time* (Hodder 1975), p.275.
6. Charles and Cherry Lindholm, *The Erotic Sorcerers* (Science Digest 1982), p.78.
7. Kenneth Grant, *Aleister Crowley and the Hidden God* (Muller 1973), p.53.
8. Barbara O'Brien, *Operators and Things* (Abacus 1976), p.129.
9. As above, p.130.

Chapter 8.
1. Dion Fortune, *The Sea Priestess* (Aquarian Press 1976), p.18.
2. Jeff Mayo, *Teach Yourself Astrology* (EUP), p.30.

3. See: Katherine Briggs, *A Dictionary of Fairies.*
4. As above.
5. E.S. Bradburne, *Opal Whiteley* (Putnam 1962), p.47.
6. Christine Hartley, *The Western Mystery Tradition* p.26.
7. *New Dimensions Red Book* (Helios 1968), p.74.
8. Jean Markale, *Women of the Celts* (G. Cremonesi), p.133.
9. Christine Hartley, *The Western Mystery Tradition* p.50.
10. Dion Fortune, *The Mystical Qabalah* (Ernest Benn), p.228.

Chapter 9.
1. Jeff Mayo, *Teach Yourself Astrology* (EUP), p.25.
2. W.G. Gray, *The Inner Traditions of Magic* (Aquarian Press), p.137.
3. Quoted from: Paul Newman's *Dragon Under the Hill* (Kingsmead 1979).
4. As above, p.58.
5. Paraphrased from *Women of the Celts*, p.175.
6. Geoffrey Ashe, *Camelot and the Vision of Albion* (Book Club Associates 1975), p.91.

Chapter 10.
1. Dion Fortune, *The Mystical Qabalah*, p.267.
2. Francis Hitching, *Earth Magic* (Cassell & Co. 1976), pp.176–7.
3. Robert Graves, *The White Goddess* (Faber 1981), p.208.

Chapter 11.
1. Lucie Lamy, *Egyptian Mysteries* (Thames & Hudson 1981), p.71.
2. Jacques Lecarriere, *The Gnostics* (Peter Own Ltd. 1977), p.17.
3. Quoted in: *The Western Mystery Tradition*, pp.24–25.
4. As above.

Index

INDEX